Promoting
Men's Health

For Siobhan

'Do not wish to be anything except what you are'

St. Francis De Sales

Table of Contents

Introduction

Introduction.

Throughout the course of history in many countries of the world, the organisation of human society has often been based on the assumption that men are the stronger, and women the weaker sex. It is only comparatively recently that this assumption has been challenged and it has been shown that on medical grounds at least, this is not true.

Studies show that being born male is a disadvantage with regard to health and life expectancy. Baby boys are more frequent victims of Sudden Infant Death Syndrome (SIDS or cot death) than girls and the life expectancy for men is only seventy-two years compared with seventy-eight years for women. In most senior age groups, over eighty years old, women outnumber men four to one.

Men are far more likely to die prematurely before reaching old age than women, falling victim to strokes, heart disease and cancer. In addition males are more likely to commit suicide or die as a result of violence or aggression.

In Ireland, excess mortality amongst males represents a fundamental inequality in health[1]. Men in Ireland die on average nearly six years younger than women do and have higher death rates at all ages and for all leading causes of death.

Whilst the issue of women's health[2] has been the source of extensive consultation and strategic planning the same cannot be said for men's health. Although men have been identified as a target population group, for the first time, in

---

[1] Balanda and Wilde 2001
[2] Department of Health and Children 1997

5

the strategic planning of health promotion and healthcare[1], there appears to have been little momentum to date to act on these initiatives.

Although research is limited in Ireland, it is well documented internationally that compared to women, men have limited contact with GPs, are reluctant users of primary care services and often present late in the course of an illness.

A survey carried out in the UK in 1997 in which eight hundred and thirty-nine men were interviewed over the telephone revealed that: thirty-one percent would delay seeing their GP until a health problem became more irritating but seventy-three per cent would like access to a men's health clinic and sixty-six per cent would like to telephone a confidential men's health advice line.[2] Similar results in the Republic of Ireland were obtained in a study by Stakelum and Boland (2001) and more recently by Richardson (2003).

This situation can be redressed through Health Promotion. Health Promotion enables and empowers individuals as well as communities to take greater control of their own health and of the quality of their lives.

The aim of this publication is to identify the need for health promotion to target male specific health issues. The author hopes to explain why this is needed and what health promotion would hope to achieve.

In the opening chapter the author will discuss the life expectancy of males and will compare the state of men's health with other countries and explore the gender differences, which possibly could contribute, to man's neglect of his health.

---

[1] Department of Health and Children 2000; 2001
[2] Carroll (1999)

6

In chapter two, the author will discuss male specific health issues. A men's health issue is a disease or condition unique to men, more prevalent in men, more serious among men, for which risk factors are different for men or for which different interventions are required for men.[1]

Chapter three will explore the issue of violence against men but in particular female violence and the negative impact it has on a man's health.

Chapter four will examine suicide in Ireland and more specifically suicide in Irish men. The chapter will review the statistics available and offer suggestions as to why eighty percent of suicides are male.

The concluding chapter will summarize the previous four chapters and offer suggestions and recommendations as to what can be done to improve men's health.

As recently as 1900 the life expectancy of men and women was about the same. Even as late as 1920 the gap was just one year but by 1998 this had increased to six years. Men are nearly twice as likely as women to die of heart disease. Men die from cancer at a rate nearly 50 percent greater than women. They are three times as likely to die of injuries or four times as likely to die of suicide or AIDS. They drown at higher rates and die at higher rates from violent crimes.

It is true that women are more likely to suffer from certain conditions than men, such as osteoporosis and immune disorders. But the loss of life, for which men are at greater risk, must be considered the greatest loss of all. As Mary Robinson, a former UN High Commissioner for Human Rights,

---

[1] Fletcher (1996)

once said, the right to life is "the most precious of rights."

Chapter 1

Life Expectancy

Introduction:

The purpose of this chapter is to explore the differences in life expectancy between men and women and compare the state of men's health in Ireland with countries in Europe. It will also contrast behavioural and biological differences between men and women. Men need to be approached differently and the values of society must change in order to encourage men to look after their health.

Traditionally the difference between men and women's health problems has been seen as relating to their sexual organs and functions but it is more complex than this. Every cell has a sex. Major studies are now generating increasing evidence on important differences between men and women, from the cellular to the societal level.

Life Expectancy.

In spite of increased male life expectancy, men continue to have higher death rates at all ages, and for all leading causes of death.[1]

In Ireland, for every seven women who are aged sixty-five years of age or over, there are five men, and amongst those who are eighty-five years of age or over, there are three women for every one man.[1]

---

[1] Richardson (2003).
[1] Murphy-Lawless (2003).

9

Life expectancy at birth provides one of the broadest indicators of the overall health of a population. Life expectancy at birth has increased, substantially for Irish men and women over the past four decades, although life expectancy is still poorer for men.

A baby boy or girl born in 1925 in the Republic of Ireland could expect, on the basis of mortality figures at that time, to live on average to about fifty-seven years of age. By contrast, the life expectancy for people born in 1996 was on average seventy-three for boys and seventy-nine for girls. Hence what was once a minor difference in life expectancy has widened into a perceptible gap of six years.

Life expectancy for males at birth in the Republic of Ireland is the third lowest in the EU and lowest of all EU countries at age sixty-five.[2] On average, Irish males can expect to live to seventy-four years, British men to seventy-five years, while Swedish men survive to seventy-seven years.[3]

In 1998, males were admitted to hospitals in the republic of Ireland more often than females for all diagnostic categories, with the notable exception of genito-urinary diseases.

Circulatory disorder, diabetes, alcoholism, duodenal ulcer and lung cancer are more common in men, while women have significantly higher rates of depression, eating and connective tissue disorders. Male suicide rates continue to exceed those in females throughout life and women survive men by several years in almost all countries and the gap is widening.

"Men have higher mortality rates for all fifteen leading causes

---

[2] Eurostat 2000; Stakelum and Boland 2001
[3] Eurostat 2000

of death" [1]

Male behaviour.

Boys are actively discouraged from seeking help by parents, other adults and peers, and indeed may be ridiculed by their peers when they do seek help. Both parents teach boy babies to perform rather than cry by picking up the male less frequently than the female infant when he cries. By the age of thirteen months, boys who are picked up less are more reluctant to seek help and refrain from crying.[2] In this way self-care practices have become culturally defined as 'feminine'. Denial of fear or vulnerability and men's late presentation to health services when they are ill, are important examples of this.

Since sickness may be seen as an expression of weakness, many men may actively decide not to seek help, and instead present a stoical, brave and unflinching front to the outside world. In order to 'prove' their own masculinity and to avoid the ridicule or stigma of being labelled feminine or effeminate some men deliberately engage in potentially compromising health behaviours.[3] It is crucial that men's health policy in the future attempts to address this very core issue.

It appears that men are less inclined than women to perceive themselves as being at risk, even in relation to risks that men are more likely to experience.[1]

The male sex stereotype demands that men be healthy, strong and self-sufficient. Often in an attempt to maintain a

---

[1] Mathers et al. (2001).
[2] Goldberg (1969).
[3] Richardson (2003).
[1] Courtenay (2000).

self-image consistent with society's expectations to be manly, men become more reluctant, not just to admit, but often recognise, their physical and mental health needs. Furthermore, men who have traditional attitudes towards masculinity are often inclined to suppress their emotions, which may partly explain the lower rate of mental health problems reported among males.[2]
A common reaction among men when this happens is to act out their emotions by engaging in fast driving, hard drinking and other risk-taking behaviours.

A man who does gender correctly would spend much time in the world away from home. The intense and active stimulation of his senses would be something he would come to depend on. He would face danger fearlessly, take risks frequently, and have little concern for his own safety.[3]

Many men fail to get routine check-ups, preventive care or health counselling, and they often ignore symptoms or delay seeking medical attention when sick or in pain.[4]
Men's Health in the European Union.

In the European Union at birth there are more boys than girls with this increased ratio lasting until the forty-five to sixty-four age bracket when the ratio of females to males becomes greater due to the increased rate of premature death in men.[1]
The male to female advantage in the early years originates from an increased number of male embryos, with approximately one-hundred and twenty male conceptions to one-hundred girls. However, due to the vulnerability of the male embryo this reduces to approximately one hundred and

---

[2] Stakelum and Boland (2001).
[3] Courtenay (1998).
[4] Mathers (2001).
[1] Eurostat (2002)

five male births to one hundred girls.[2] Across the European Union there has been a higher proportion of boys born to girls: between 1980 and 1999 51.6% of babies born were boys as compared to 48.4% girls.[3]

In the majority of countries there are a greater number of young men in relation to men over the age of sixty-five. The country with the largest percentage of young men is Ireland (23%) as compared to Italy where there are an equal number of young men to older men. [4]

The projected increases in life expectancy figures suggest that men's life expectancy will continue to increase at a faster rate than women. The figures also suggest, however that the life expectancy for men in twenty years time will still be less than that of women currently and is only just reaching the figures for women in the 1980's.[5]

Men have a greater risk of premature death than women, although the risk varies between different countries. Portugal has the largest number of years lost as a result of premature death in men under the age of sixty-five years with seven years lost, with Sweden having the lowest (four years), but they still have more years lost than the women in all the countries.[6]

Males have a higher rate of death than females throughout the age span. [7]Following birth boys are at a greater risk of death within the first year with the proportion of deaths in the EU among babies in their first year four per thousand

---

[2] Shettles (1961).
[3] Eurostat (2002).
[4] Health for All Database (2003).
[5] World Health Report (2002).
[6] HFA (2003).
[7] Kraemer (2000).

girls and five per thousand boys, which equates to over fifty-six percent of deaths of babies before they reach their first birthday.[1]

Once boys enter childhood (between the ages of one to fourteen) they again are seen to have a greater risk of dying with a median death rate per hundred thousand of forty-nine for boys and thirty-eight for girls. Portugal is seen to have a marked greater risk than the other countries.[2]
For adult male death rates continue to be higher than females for each age bracket.

Cardio-vascular disease is the principal cause of death in men with a median death rate of three hundred and fifty-one per hundred thousand across all seventeen countries, followed by death due to neoplasms (with a median rate of two hundred and forty-eight deaths per hundred thousand).[3]

For young men the key causes of death were found in the external causes and poisoning category with over sixty percent of deaths between the ages of one to twenty-four years, which includes transport accidents, suicide, death by violence and other external causes.[4]

For men aged between twenty-five and sixty-four neoplasms were the main cause of death, (with thirty-six percent of the total deaths in this age bracket) followed by diseases of the circulatory system and external causes of injury and poisoning.

For men over seventy-five years cardiovascular disease becomes the major cause of death with nearly forty-five

---

[1] Eurostat (2002).
[2] WHO (1999).
[3] Eurostat (2002).
[4] Eurostat (2000).

percent of the total deaths in men.

The State of Men's Health in England and Wales is similar to that of Ireland. In the last thirty years, suicide rates in young men have more than doubled, the incidence of prostate cancer has increased by one-hundred and thirty-five percent, the number of deaths from chronic liver disease in men aged between twenty-five and sixty-four years has increased five-fold and the proportion of men who are obese has more than tripled.[1]

Sex Differences

The term gender refers to femininity and masculinity in a social or psychological sense and is distinguished from male and female in a biological sense.[2]

Gender identity refers to the way in which people view themselves along feminine/masculine lines. There are two parts to this. The first is basic gender identification or the cognitive knowledge that one is male or female.

> *"By the age of two, most children have established their basic gender identification".*[3]

The second is gender-role identity or the nature of the view of the self as a male or female in society.[4] For example a person may know himself to be a male (basic gender identification) but view himself as somewhat feminine (gender role identity).

Gender role refers to the ways in which males and females behave (or are expected to behave) in society. In the

---

[1] Baker (2004).
[2] Lindsey (1990).
[3] Money and Erhardt (1972).
[4] Kagan (1964).

Western World for example, males traditionally are expected to behave in a logical, competitive, and ambitious way, while females traditionally are expected to behave in a gentle, sensitive, and warm manner.[5]

Gender-related personality traits and temperaments refer to the underlying dispositions and emotional characteristics distinguishing males from females.

Sex is the physical difference between men and women and is influenced by genes and biology. Gender is the psychological difference in which environmental and psychological factors have a prominent role.

Biological Differences

The one biological difference between the sexes on which everybody is agreed is that whereas women possess two X-shaped sex chromosomes, men possess one X and a smaller Y-shaped chromosome. The Y chromosome accounts for superior male strength, stature, and mass of muscle, sleight of hand, speed of foot.

In every human cell there are forty-six chromosomes. Forty-four are identical pairs, but two are different- one X-shaped and one Y-shaped. These two chromosomes regulate sexual development.

Females normally have two X shaped sex chromosomes; males have one X and one Y. Under a microscope the Y chromosome appears about one-third the size of the X. It is the Y that holds the key to maleness. Without it the embryo develops as a female.

---

[5] Broverman et al. (1972).

Masculine differentiation occurs because the foetal testes, which are actively producing androgen (testosterone) and a substance that inhibits the development of the female anlagen (Mullerian inhibiting substance), impose masculinity upon the basic feminine trend of the body, whereas female differentiation proceeds in the relative absence of these influences.

So from the very outset one of the oldest explanations of the creation of the species, namely the story of Genesis in the bible, appears to get it wrong. Eve is not fashioned out of Adam's rib. Adam is made out of Eve. To be a male not only demands a Y chromosome but that a switch is turned on by one of the genes on the Y. If the switch fails then, y or no Y, the embryo turns out female.

Behavioural Differences.

While girls are taught by their mothers about their bodies, and tend to have regular contact with health services through reproductive exams (menstruation, child-bearing and menopause), boys on the other hand tend to be left to their own devices. As a result, boys tend not to develop self-nurturing attitudes and behaviours in the same way that girls do. Health needs to occupy a more prominent part of boy's school curriculum in the future.

From the moment a baby is born, parents tend to treat boys and girls differently. Although male and female babies exhibit few behavioural differences, most parents will describe their daughters as cuter, softer or more delicate than their sons. Fathers are especially likely to treat babies differently based on gender. Fathers tend to emphasise the beauty and delicacy of their newborn daughters and the strength and coordination of their newborn sons.[1]

From the beginning one is treated differently according to gender. One is not only treated differently but is different and will view one another as being different. This philosophy of thinking dates back to Aristotle when he claims that women were *"more compassionate.... more envious, more querulous, more slanderous, and more contentious"* and that men were *"more disposed to give assistance in danger and more courageous"*. He believed that these were natural female and male traits; not characteristics that were taught or learned.

Men are slower to notice signs of illness, and when they do, they are less likely than women to seek help from a doctor and are more likely to play down their symptoms.[1] When men go to their doctor, they take much less physician time than women do, receiving less information with fewer and briefer explanations.[2] We need to explore fully how men interact with health services, and how health services can be made more amenable and accessible to men in the future.

The literature around mental and emotional health suggests that men are much more likely than women to focus on physical problems and less likely to report concerns relating to mental or emotional problems.[3] Challenging some of the traditional taboos around mental health is critically important in terms of moving mental health issues for men forward at a policy level.

The roles of men and women are changing, but according to a recent report on men's health, males "continue to be

---

[1] Krieger (1976).
[1] Kraemer (2000).
[2] Richardson (2003).
[3] Stakelum and Boland (2001).

socialised to appear in control, to be strong and to take risks; thus reinforcing their exposure to illness and accidental deaths." The problems associated with risk-taking behaviour highlighted by the report seem to be particularly pertinent when coupled with the much higher numbers of male fatalities in road traffic accidents contained in the document. The association, too, of sickness with weakness means that men are often less likely to seek help- which results in the loss of early intervention which is critical in the treatment of most serious illnesses.

The women's movement is thirty years ahead of men. It has produced numerous journals devoted to women's health. Men's health issues in the meantime are hardly represented, not least of all in a single multidisciplinary journal.

"The health of both sexes is influenced by biological factors including, but not confined to, their reproductive characteristics".[1]

Social and Work Differences

It is true that men are more aggressive than women are. However the difference is very minute.[2] Sex differences are larger for physical aggression than for psychological or verbal aggression. Violence and aggression will be discussed in greater detail in chapter three.

Extensive observations suggest that women are more skilled and more involved in interpersonal communication than are men. The difference is particularly strong in non-verbal forms of communication. In transmitting messages non-verbally, women are more effective than men. They code their intended messages more efficiently and they transmit them

---

[1] Doyal (2001).
[2] Eagly (1987); Hyde (1986).

to partners more effectively. They also smile significantly more when talking to others, and they spend more time gazing at their conversational partners.[3]
Overall, women are more easily influenced than men are. Differences between women and men are more pronounced when other people are present, suggesting the influence of gender-linked norms.[4] According to Deaux (1984) females conform more than males in group pressure situations, they are more susceptible to persuasion. Deaux also states that women are better able to decode non-verbal messages.

The two sexes tend to use very different vocabulary. Lakoff (1973) claims that women's language contains more intensifiers (very, extremely etc.), qualifiers/hedges (I suppose, I guess, maybe), and tag questions than does men's speech. This, Lakoff argues, leads to women's speech being seen as less powerful than the speech style typically produced by men. Women also tend to have less control over the conversation than men.[1]

Men tend to focus more on the goal-directed, task features of a situation, whereas women contribute to the socio-emotional climate. Sex differences in group interaction are most likely when it is unclear how competent other group members are. In such circumstances, gender acts as an implied status characteristic, and men are assumed to have greater competence than women do. For similar reasons, men are more likely to emerge as leaders in initially leaderless groups. Men are most likely to be chosen, as leaders when the group is focused on a specific task and when social interaction needs are minimal. [2]

---

[3] Hall and Halberstadt (1986).
[4] Eagly (1987).
[1] Deaux (1984).
[2] Eagly (1987).

Deaux and Major (1987) suggest the basic repertoires of women and men are quite similar, particularly when it comes to social behaviours. Both women and men know how to be aggressive, how to be helpful, how to smile, and how to be rude. What the sexes actually do is determined less by differential abilities than by the context in which they are acting.

Whereas men are more aggressive the female is more persuasive. She is the communicator, the comforter. It has been proven that women are superior in interpersonal skills.[1]

Sociolinguist Deborah Tannen suggests that men and women speak different languages. Psychologist John Gray claims that they look for different things in personal relationships. Management experts Marilyn Loden and Judy Rosener argue that they prefer different management styles. And moral development psychologist Carol Gilligan argues that they even think differently about right and wrong.

Most male managers for example, seem to prefer a leadership style based on authority, while most female managers seem more comfortable with building consensus.

For a variety of reasons whether conscious or unconscious most men experience life as a contest, battle or struggle. Most of the people around them are experienced as opponents, adversaries – even enemies. "Winning" or "losing" always hangs in the balance. Life is; in essence, viewed as a struggle.

Most women, by contrast, live in a less threatening world. Experts claim that, consciously and /or unconsciously, the majority of women are driven more to form relationships with

---

[1] Hall and Halberstadt, 1986

other people than to defeat them. These women see other people as partners and friends not foes. And they seek intimacy with them. Most women experience life in a way that is comparable to living in a community where the lives and interests of all of its members are intimately connected. For most women then, life isn't a contest, but a community where conflict must be avoided.

Work primarily to the female is less about winning than about working together to achieve a common goal. The feminine belief is that business operates best if people co-operate with, not compete against one another. The female attitude is that people around them are allies to be empowered and not adversaries to be bested. Work is about being involved in achieving something that the group believes is important.

Women see the workplace as something akin to a village square. This would explain why they usually emphasise consensus-building, involving many people in any decision, getting people to buy in to any new programme and making sure that everyone understands the rationale behind any significant decision or policy.

Women in general behave differently at meetings than men do. Women tend to be relatively quiet at meetings, listening more than they speak. They press their own point of view less aggressively than men do. Women are not policy people. They are generally willing to make exceptions to policies and to adopt an ad hoc approach to problems. They prefer more participatory forms of management. They prefer "horizontal Management" allowing decisions to be made at low levels of responsibility and empowering subordinates,

They usually arrange their office furniture so that there are no barriers like desks between themselves and other people. They prefer egalitarian arrangements: movable furniture, chairs in circle, tables without "power positions" and the like.

As a result of the different behaviours at work, men place themselves under more stress and further increase their risk of diseases associated with stress such as heart disease and stroke.

Summary

The life-span gender gap exists in almost every country in the world. The disparity ranges from four years in Israel to fifteen years in the Russian Federation. This disparity is expected to worsen. According to the WHO Global Burden of Disease study, women's life expectancy is expected to increase to about ninety years by 2020 in industrialized countries. As for men, "far smaller gains in male life expectancy were projected than in females".

The greatest disparities are found between the ages of fifteen to sixty, the years when people are most productive to society. According to the Global Burden of Disease Study, male mortality in this critical age group surpassed female deaths by substantial margins in all eight regions of the world.

In the industrialized countries of North America and Europe, there are twice as many male deaths as female deaths among people aged between fifteen and sixty years old. In the former Soviet countries of Eastern Europe, the gender disparity in this age group is greater than two to one.

All around the world, the life span of men lags behind that of women. This generalization applies to the three major categories of death, in virtually every country, and in all age groups.

A gendered approach distinguishes between sex (being male) and gender (living as masculine in a particular culture), in examining 'men's health' issues. In the case of many health issues, both are inextricably linked. For example, whilst prostate and testicular cancer are unequivocally sex-specific conditions, they become gender -specific in the way that many men present late to their doctor with symptoms, or in the way that they subsequently cope with their illness. A gendered approach to men's health therefore is crucial in the context of men's health policy development in the future.

Long-term polices and strategies that adopt a gendered approach to men's health are much more likely to succeed than a knee-jerk reaction approach to specific male health issues.

"A gender-blind approach to health and healthcare serves neither men nor women well" Donna Stewart
Donna Stewart chaired the committee that prepared the Canadian Institute for Health Information Report

There has been a culture of strategic planning and provision around women's health throughout the history of the state- beginning with Dr. Noel Browne, minister for health in the first coalition government, who pressed for the introduction of a Mother and Child Scheme. While there is no doubt that this Scheme and the reasons for its conception were warranted, no similar attempts were made, or have been since, to highlight the different requirements of men's health and the type of healthcare provision they need.

It is a feature of western medicine in general that (outside the field of gynaecology) it rarely differentiates between genders. As concerns in Ireland grow over issues such as young male suicide and the rise in reported numbers of cases of prostate and testicular cancer, the time has come for the medical profession and the government to question the validity of this approach.

Men not just in Ireland but internationally, are less likely to visit a GP at the beginning stages of illness or indeed at all.

Health services across the country do not seem to be making the same effort to encourage men into the doctor's surgery.

The following chapter will focus on male specific health issues and in particular that of cancer of specific organs. In most cases of cancer, if the disease is detected early, the outcome is better. There is therefore an urgency to encourage and educate men to be aware of the various signs and symptoms.

Chapter 2

Male Specific Health issues.

Introduction.

A men's health issue is a disease or condition unique to men, more prevalent in men, more serious among men, for which risk factors are different for men or for which different interventions are required for men. [1]

It is any issue, condition or determinant that affects the quality of life of men and/or which different responses are required in order for men (and boys) to experience optimal social, emotional and physical health.[2]

The purpose of this chapter is to outline male specific health issues that can result in death when not detected in time. The majority of these issues are cancer of a specific organ.

There are many different types of cancer, each of which involves unrestrained growth of cells inside a specific organ or tissue in the body. The most common types of cancer in men are lung, skin, large bowel, prostate and testicular cancer. Stomach, pancreas and bladder cancers are also principal causes of death in men.

In 2001 the leading causes of death among men in Ireland (in order of the number of deaths) were circulatory diseases (40%), cancers (27%) and respiratory diseases (13%).[3] Overall, men and women had similar risks of developing cancer although men were more likely to die from it.

---

[1] Fletcher (1996)
[2] New South Wales Health Department (1999)
[3] Health Statistics (2002)

26

Estimated lifetime risks of developing malignant cancer were about one in three for both men and women. The risk of dying from malignant cancer before the age of seventy-five was about one in eight for women, but about one in six for men. [1]
In 1998, 28.5%, of male deaths in Europe were attributed to malignant neoplasms compared to 22% for female deaths.[2]

By being aware of the warning symptoms of cancer, regular examination of skin and testicles for abnormal changes and visiting one's doctor if there are warning signals, the diagnosis can be confirmed at the earliest possible stage which will give subsequent treatment a greater chance of success.

In recent years there have been a number of advances in cancer treatment, with improvements in surgical and radiotherapy techniques and a wider variety of more effective anti-cancer drugs. Men who delay seeking medical help miss out on potentially life-saving therapies.

This chapter will describe briefly the specific cancers that affect men and demonstrate how early intervention saves lives. Early intervention can only be achieved through education through health promotion.

Prostate

Anatomically the prostate is a small gland situated below and behind the bladder in the male. Its function is to aid in the production of seminal fluid. Urine passes from the bladder through the urethra in the centre of the prostate then down

---

[1] National Cancer Registry Board (2001).
[2] Eurostat 2000

through the penis. From the age of forty the prostate gland increases in size. There are two reasons for prostate enlargement, benign prostatic hyperplasia caused by normal male hormones and carcinoma of the prostate.

When the prostate enlarges the urethra becomes narrowed. The prostate needs to be treated to relieve difficulty-passing urine and to prevent complete blockage. If the blockage continues for a prolonged period due to retention of urine, damage to the kidneys and bladder may occur

In 1998, the Republic of Ireland ranked sixth amongst fellow EU countries in terms of standardised death rates due to cancer of the prostate (32 per 100,000). Sweden ranked the highest with a rate of 39 per 100,000 and Greece the lowest with a rate of 16 per 100,000.[1]

Nature hid the prostate gland and most people seem content to leave it at that.[2] So little attention is paid to this gland that not only does the average male often mistake the word as prostrate but often high profile members of the media as well.

According to O' Dowd et al. (2002), very few countries collect healthcare information on non-malignant prostatic disease that could be used to help estimate a more accurate figure of the number of men with this condition. The Netherlands is the exception. Most countries, however, which took part in the study, could provide actual figures of the incidence of malignant disease.

In a European study carried out by O' Dowd et al (2002), findings show that there was an abundance of clinically

---

[1] Eurostat (2000).
[2] Bulla (2003).

related information for benign prostatic hyperplasia (BPH). However, there is very little patient-focussed, qualitative research that looks at the morbidity of non-malignant prostatic disease and the impact it has on men's lives and the lives of their family members.

Benign Prostatic Hyperplasia

The majority of men who develop a prostate problem suffer from a benign enlargement of their prostate gland, known medically as benign prostatic hyperplasia (BPH) meaning an increase in the number of cells within the prostate gland. Benign prostatic hyperplasia is a condition ten times more common than prostate cancer. One in ten men affected will require surgery.

While it is normal for the prostate gland to enlarge around the time of puberty as part of male sexual development, it is not understood why it should start growing again in so many men once they pass the age of fifty.

Because of the glands position just underneath the bladder and surrounding the upper part of the urethra (the narrow tube that carries urine and semen to the tip of the penis), prostate enlargement may interfere with the normal flow of urine.

Until recently, the symptoms of BPH were attributed primarily to physical pressure exerted by the enlarged prostate gland on the urethra. It is now realised that symptoms are also the result of an increase in smooth muscle tone in both the prostate and neck of the bladder.

This explains why the severity of symptoms is not necessarily related to the size of the prostate gland. Minimal enlargement of the prostate may cause severe urinary problems that significantly disrupt daytime activities with sleep, while a large prostate may cause only minimal disability.

The characteristic symptoms of an enlarged prostate are difficulty in starting the flow of urine, a weak stream that may stop and start several times, a feeling that the bladder hasn't been completely emptied, frequent need to urinate, finding it difficult to postpone urination and needing to urinate at intervals throughout the night and dribbling after urination.

As a result of these symptoms benign prostatic hyperplasia may have a major impact on a man's quality of life. He may have to restrict his intake of fluids before travelling anywhere without toilets nearby, disturb his and his partners sleep, or be embarrassed by episodes of incontinence.

Men delay seeing a doctor until their symptoms have become intolerable, either because they are too embarrassed, or because they mistakenly think that their problem is an inevitable part of growing old. Treatment is usually successful in restoring near-normal urinary function.

To confirm that the prostate gland is enlarged, the doctor may perform a digital rectal examination, whereby a lubricated gloved finger is inserted in to the rectum and the prostate palpated through the front wall of the rectum, which lies against the back of the gland.

Most men suffering from benign prostatic hyperplasia can now be effectively managed by drug treatment. If medical treatment does not provide sufficient symptom relief or if complications have developed, such as recurrent urine infection, bladder stones, retention of urine in the bladder or kidney damage resulting from back pressure, the man will usually be referred for a surgical procedure.

Surgery for BPH usually involves a trans-urethral resection of the prostate (TURP), in which a long narrow instrument (resectoscope) is passed up the urethra towards the bladder. At the tip of the resectoscope is an electrically heated wire loop that is used to shave away the obstructing prostate tissue, while the surgeon watches the procedure through a small telescope contained within the instrument.

TURP should make no difference to male libido, but it may occasionally cause impotence as a psychological response, particularly in men who haven't been properly counselled before their operation.

Prostatitis.

Prostatitis is a condition in which the prostate gland becomes inflamed, usually due to a bacterial infection that has spread from the urethra.

It is most common in men between the ages of 20 and 40 years. The infection may be sexually transmitted or develop as a complication of a urinary tract infection. Prostatitis in which no infection is found may be due to irritation of the prostate gland from the reflux of urine as a result of tiny stones forming within the gland ducts.

Symptoms of prostatitis may include pain or frequency passing urine, fever, low back pain; deep pain felt between the scrotum and the anus, discharge from the penis and sometimes pain on ejaculation.

Diagnosis may be confirmed by rectal examination, in which the doctor inserts a lubricated-gloved finger into the rectum to feel the prostate gland through the front wall. The prostate will characteristically feel tender and swollen. To establish whether a particular bug is causing the inflammation, a sample of urine may be sent to the laboratory for analysis, along with a sample of urethral secretions, obtained after massaging the prostate gland during the rectal examination.

If Prostatitis is due to a bacterial infection, treatment is with a prolonged course of antibiotics. Non-bacterial prostatitis may be treated with anti-inflammatory painkillers such as ibuprofen. Symptoms may persist for several months and also tend to recur.

Cancer of the Prostate

1150 new cases of prostate cancer are diagnosed in Ireland each year, with one man in eleven developing prostate cancer at some time during his life. The annual death rate from prostate cancer in Ireland is 513.[1]

During 1989-1998 an average of nearly seven hundred men died each year on the island from malignant neoplasms of the prostate.

In neither Northern Ireland nor the Republic of Ireland was there a significant difference in the annual directly standardised mortality rate of the highest and lowest occupational classes.[2]

Prostate cancers occur mainly in elderly men, with half of all cases occurring in men over the age of seventy-five years. Nearly all deaths due to prostate cancer have occurred in men aged over sixty-five years.

Prostate cancer is one of the most common types of cancer in men and the second most common cause of cancer death in men. Seven times as many men die from prostate cancer as

---

[1] National Cancer Registry Board (2001).
[2] Balanda and Wilde (2001).

women die from cervical cancer. [3]

The exact cause of prostate cancer remains unknown. Several risk factors have been identified. A man with an affected brother or father is eight times more likely to develop prostate cancer than a man without a similar family history. Large intake of saturated fat in one's diet may also increase the risk.

Prostate cancer not only kills but also causes distressing symptoms. Pressure from the tumour on the bladder and its outlet, the urethra may cause difficulty and pain passing urine.

In most cases cancer of the prostate does not produce any symptoms until it has already spread to other parts of the body. Screening for prostate cancer before it causes symptoms may be done by a simple blood test to measure the level of the protein prostate specific antigen (PSA), and by a digital rectal examination, whereby the doctor inserts a gloved, lubricated finger into the rectum to feel whether the prostate has become abnormally hard or knobbly.

The incidence of prostate cancer increases with age, however prostate cancer can be asymptomatic until late into the disease. A man over fifty presenting with low back pain will sometimes be found to have bone secondaries of the pelvis and sacrum with the primary cancer eventually traced to the prostate gland.

Treatment of Prostate Cancer

Treatment of the cancer involves resection of the tumour if it is caught early on. The procedure is similar to that commonly

---

[3] Health Statistics 2002

called a TURP (Transurethral resection of the prostate). The surgeon passes a telescope through the inside of the penis into the bladder. The blockage can be observed and cut away. These pieces of prostate are removed and sent to the pathologist for examination. A catheter is left in situ to drain away any exudate. Post operatively the area bleeds for a few days. Fluid is flushed in and out of the catheter to stop it from becoming blocked with a blood clot. The catheter is removed when the bleeding stops.

Hormonal treatment (a form of chemotherapy) can also be given which is aimed at suppressing the body's production of testosterone. Prostate cancer thrives on testosterone, the male hormone. Radiotherapy is used to shrink any bone secondaries and occasionally the testicles are removed to further reduce testosterone levels.

Because it is often a late diagnosis, the disease is allowed time to establish itself hence the need for increased awareness and vigilance towards this killer.

All men over forty should have an annual examination by a GP who will refer them on to a urologist if necessary. Assessment has been helped by the development of a blood test the PSA. This measures a substance called the prostate specific antigen. The normal levels in the blood are up to four. A reading between four and ten could be due to other causes such as infection or benign enlargement. A PSA reading of greater that ten however warrants further investigation. Prostate cancer can be successfully treated if it is diagnosed early.

Research shows that very little work has been done to look at the psychological and social aspects of diseases of the prostate that may affect one in four men at some stage of their lives.

"I saw big strong men who were garrulous and full of jokes

about the "waterworks department" when they arrived. When they left with nothing but a plastic bag of elephantine nappies under their arm, I saw broken men who didn't know how to cope," .[1]

O Dowd et al (2002) also noted a significant shortage of urologists or prostatic disease specialists in the republic of Ireland, which suggest that Irish men could be denied access to the treatments they need. The study found that there were only twenty-three urologists in the republic of Ireland, representing a rate of 3.2 specialists per 100,000 males aged forty and over.

Even though prostatic cancer killed nine-hundred Irish men in 2002, there is no prostatic screening in Ireland. Furthermore, although sixty-five radical prostatectomies were carried out in 2002 the department of Health and our hospital administration do not think this value for money, and have now closed all our urology beds (except day beds) in order to balance their books.[2]

Testicular Cancer

One in every two hundred and seventy-three men will develop testicular cancer; some needlessly die from it each year because of failure to detect it in time.[3]

Testicular tumours are the most common tumours in males aged between twenty and forty. In males of all ages they comprise about one per cent of all malignancies.

Mal-descended testes are at least thirty times more likely to become malignant than normally descended testes. These

---

[1] Cahill (2002).
[2] Smith (2003).
[3] Armstrong 2001

tumours are characterised both by their rapid growth and sensitivity to chemotherapy or radiotherapy.

There is a ninety-five per cent cure rate if detected early. However in men presenting with secondaries the cure rate is fifty percent. An awareness of this disease among young men is essential and will improve early detection rates.

Malignant testicular tumours usually present as a painless progressively enlarging testicle. A testicular lump must be assumed to be a tumour until proven otherwise. With testicular cancer early diagnosis means a better outcome.

While cancer of one of the testicles is very rare before puberty and in old age, it is the most common cancer in men between the ages of fifteen and forty-nine years and is the fourth biggest killer of men aged fifteen to thirty-four.[1]

Testicular cancer is not a key cause of death in men, however it has a specific relevance as it affects young men and it has such a high potential cure rate. It also has great emotive importance as it concerns the male genitalia and is one of the few male specific illnesses.

There has been a substantial reduction in death rates for testicular cancer across all countries over the last twenty-five years. The scale of the decrease ranges from thirty-one percent in Spain to eighty-three percent in Sweden.[2]

However the incidence of testicular cancer has doubled since the 1970's.

The reason for this increase is unknown. If diagnosed early over ninety percent of testicular cancer can be cured and

---

[1] National Cancer Registry (2002).
[2] Eurostat (2002).

providing the remaining testicle is healthy, treatment should not interfere with fertility or potency. Regular self-examination of the testicles is therefore essential to allow early diagnosis.

Early signs include a swelling, lump, or dull ache in the scrotal area. Stomach or backache can also be a symptom, suggesting the cancer could be spreading.

Testicular cancer has become much more common in the last fifty years. One theory is that environmental pollutants and foodstuffs (particularly cow's milk) containing oestrogen have affected the development of the male while still in his mother's womb.

There are two main types of tumour - a seminoma (which mostly affects thirty to forty year-olds) and a teratoma (mostly affecting twenty to thirty year-olds). The affected testicle is almost always removed but seminomas are usually also treated with radiotherapy and teratomas with chemotherapy. Chemotherapy can be used for seminomas if the cancer has spread beyond the testicles.

Many men put themselves at greater risk by waiting too long before seeing a doctor. About half of all cases are undetected until the tumour has spread to other organs.

Despite attempts by various members of the media to raise awareness of this condition there appears to be a huge reluctance among both the male and female populations in recognising this issue.

Colon Cancer

The third most common type of cancer in men affects the colon or rectum. Five hundred and seventy-two new cases of men affected with the disease are reported in Ireland each year with an annual death rate in men of three hundred and seventy. This form of cancer usually develops between the ages of fifty and seventy years.

During 1989-1998 an average of over one thousand people died each year on the island from malignant neoplasms of the colon. The all Ireland annual directly standardised mortality rate was significantly higher for males than it was for females (forty-five percent higher).[1]

In both Northern Ireland and the Republic of Ireland the annual directly standardised mortality rate in the lowest occupational class was significantly (over fifty percent) higher than the rate in the highest occupational class.

The proportion of total deaths due to cancer of the colon in the EU range from 1.1% in Finland to 2.4% in The Netherlands.

Cancer of the colon is primarily a problem for men over the age of sixty-five in all the countries with the largest proportion of deaths occurring in the over seventy-five's.

Comparison with women shows that across the different age brackets men have a higher rate of death than women.

The incidence rates for cancer of the colon and rectum combined show Germany and Ireland have the highest new cases with nearly 45 new cases per 100,000 population.[2]

When the incidence for men and women are compared men have a consistently higher number of new cases per year than women.

Colon Cancer is a disease in which cancer (malignant) cells

---

[1] Balanda & Wilde (2000).
[2] Globocan (2000).

are found in the tissues of the colon. The colon is part of the body's digestive system. The purpose of the digestive system is to remove nutrients (vitamins, minerals, carbohydrates, fats, proteins, and water) from the foods eaten and to store the waste until it passes out of the body. The digestive system is made up of the oesophagus, stomach, and the small and large intestines. The last six feet of intestine is called the large bowel or colon.

The exact cause of large bowel cancer is unknown but genetic and dietary factors are believed to play an important part. Risk factors include : eating a high-meat, high fat, low-fibre diet, and suffering from either ulcerative colitis or familial polyposis coli, an inherited disorder which causes hundred of polyps (small growths) in the colon lining.

Symptoms of this particular cancer may include a prolonged change from one's normal bowel habit, such as constipation or diarrhoea lasting more than ten days, blood mixed with one's stools and the sensation of not being able to empty bowels completely.

Radiotherapy or anti cancer drugs may be used to treat large bowel cancer, in addition to surgical removal of the tumour. It may be necessary for the surgeon to create a temporary or even a permanent colostomy where the cut end of the colon is brought to the surface of the skin and the faeces empty into a bag attached to the front of the abdomen.

Surgery is the most common treatment of all stages of cancer of the colon. If the cancer is at a very early stage, the cancer may be removed without cutting into the abdomen. Instead a catheter is inserted through the rectum into the colon and the tumour removed. This is called a local excision. If the cancer is found in a small bulging piece of tissue (called a polyp), the operation is called a polypectomy.

If the cancer is larger, the cancer and a small amount of

healthy tissue around it (bowel or colon resection) are removed. The healthy parts of the colon are then sewn together (anastomosis). Lymph nodes near the intestine are removed and examined.

If the surgeon is unable to reunite the colon, a colostomy is created. When the entire lower colon is removed the colostomy is permanent.
About half of the people who have surgery for rectal cancer survive for at least three years after the operation and forty-five percent are alive ten years later.

Radiation therapy is the use of x-rays or other high-energy rays to kill cancer cells and shrink tumours. There are two types of radiation therapy, external and internal. Internal is the induction of radioactive materials into the intestine area. Radiation can be used alone or in addition to surgery and/or chemotherapy.

Chemotherapy is the use of drugs to kill cancer cells. Chemotherapy may be taken orally, or intravenously. A patient may be given chemotherapy through a catheter that is left in the vein while a small pump gives the patient constant treatment over a period of weeks. Chemotherapy is called a systemic treatment because the drug enters the bloodstream, travels through the body, and can kill cancer cells outside the colon. If the cancer has spread to the liver, the patient may be given chemotherapy directly into the hepatic artery.

If all the cancer that can be seen is removed at the time of the operation, the patient may be given chemotherapy after surgery to kill any cancer cells that are left. Chemotherapy given after an operation to a person who has no cancer cells that can be seen is called adjuvant chemotherapy.

Biological treatment uses materials made by the body or made in a laboratory to boost, direct, or restore the body's natural defences against disease.

As with most cancers colon cancer can be successfully treated if it is diagnosed early.

Haemophilia

Haemophilia is an inherited bleeding disorder in which there is a lifelong deficiency of one of the essential blood clotting factors. It's a sex linked recessive condition meaning that the gene for haemophilia is found on the X chromosome and that only males are affected.

There are different types of the condition and varying levels of severity.

Haemophilia A results from a deficiency in levels of Factor VIII. This is the most common type, affecting 1 in 10,000 males. Haemophilia B is caused by a deficiency of Factor IX and affects 1 in 100,000 males.[*] Both Haemophilia A and B are clinically identical, only blood tests can differentiate them. The level of the relevant clotting factor in the blood will dictate the severity of the condition.

Haemophilia Treatment

In Ireland there are approximately two hundred men and eighty-five boys with severe haemophilia. Several hundred more have mild and moderate versions of the condition. Haemophilia is treated by administration of the missing clotting factor to elevate the patient's circulating levels up to or close to normal. In 1965 cryoprecipitate was discovered. This substance, rich in factor VIII, appeared on the surface of slowly thawed plasma. The rapid administration of a large and precisely known amount of coagulation factor, in a small

---

[*] NCHD (2004).

volume, was possible and this discovery led to the advent of home treatment.

It is now recognised that this introduced the potential for the transmission of viruses. Large numbers of patients around the world were infected with HIV between 1979- 1985. The hepatitis C virus was identified in 1989 and it soon became clear that an even higher proportion of men with haemophilia had been exposed to this virus. Since that time, viral-inactivation treatments of factor concentrates using heat or detergents have become standard practice, vastly improving the safety of such products.

In 1984 sequencing of the gene for factor VIII was developed. This led to the availability of genetically engineered factor VIII and the availability of genetically engineered factor IX also known as recombinant in 1997. These products are now widely used in the developed world for prophylactic regimes, which aim to prevent bleeding episodes as well as the treatment of acute bleeding episodes.

Socio Economic Factors

There are differences in death rates across the social economic groups for each age category, particularly in the older age categories. Differences are particularly evident in the fifty-five to sixty-four age bracket, where rates in the unskilled group, at twenty-two per thousand, are almost three times higher than the rate for the higher professionals, at eight per thousand population. Taking all deaths in the fifteen to sixty-four age range, men in the 'unknown' category have death rates almost five times greater than men in the lower professional category.

The European Health Report 2002 reaffirms the view that all major determinants of health are linked to social and economic factors. It reports on the widening gap in health between the richest and poorest of the fifty-one European states. It reports that the biggest contributor to the worsening figures is due largely to the premature mortality among adult males.

In the United Kingdom a report "Tackling health inequalities" in 2002, noted an eight-year difference in life expectancy between men living in the affluent areas of London and the city of Manchester.

Summary

In a broader context, there is very little research that looks at specific issues in relation to men's health including their health seeing and coping strategies and how they view health. [1]

Every year over a thousand men die from prostate, colon and testicular cancer. The tragedy is that many of these lives could have been saved with early intervention. There are efforts to raise awareness of these specific issues but a lot more needs to be done or consequently more male lives will be needlessly lost and further families will be left without a father, brother, husband or son.

The following chapter will explore the issue of violence against men.
"Little is known about the needs of men who are victims of domestic violence. These groups of men, in the main, suffer in silence, ostracised by a society that still refuses to accept that women too can be perpetrators of violence." Stakeulum and Boland (2001).

For many years this was a problem that was not taken

---

[1] O' Dowd et al (2002).

seriously. Violence against men is a grave issue that has a detrimental effect on man's physical and emotional health.

Chapter Three

Violence against men.

Introduction.

People of all socio-economic classes, races, religions, ethnic backgrounds, genders and sexual orientations can be victims of domestic violence. The idea of men being abused by women runs contrary to many of society's traditional beliefs, however female violence is a well-documented phenomenon. This chapter will discuss the issue of violence against men but in particular female violence and the negative impact it has on a man's health.

Domestic Violence.

Domestic violence has been defined as any form of physical, psychological or sexual abuse, which puts the safety, or welfare of a family member at risk. It is a learned pattern of physical, verbal, sexual and or emotional behaviour in which one person in a relationship uses force and intimidation to dominate or control the other person. Domestic violence is an ongoing, debilitating experience of physical, psychological and/or sexual abuse. The violence may not happen on a daily basis, but it remains as a hidden terrorising factor. Domestic violence is not a gender issue but a social issue affecting men, women and children.[1]

The Marriage and Relationship Counselling Service (MRCS)

---

[1] Cleary (2004).

report, based on a survey of five hundred and thirty clients, found that, where domestic violence occurs, mutual violence accounts for thirty-three percent of cases, female perpetrated violence accounts for forty-one percent and male perpetrated violence for twenty-six percent. Similarly the ACCORD research, based on a survey of fifteen hundred clients, found that women were perpetrators in thirty percent of domestic violence cases, men were perpetrators in twenty-three percent of cases and mutual violence accounted for forty-eight percent. The Department of Health and Children has also carried out research, which vindicates the MRCS and ACCORD.

Physical Violence

Physical violence is an attack on the body of another person for the purpose of causing pain and injury. Physical assaults range from slapping or hitting at one end of the continuum to murder at the other extreme. It can also involve being pushed, shoved, punched, stabbed, attacked with weapons or implements, having tufts of hair pulled out, being burned or scalded. Injuries include concussion, lacerations, dislocation of joints, loss of teeth, fractures, abrasions, stabbing, scratches and cigarette burns. Women make up for their lack of physical size by using the element of surprise. Men are attacked when most vulnerable, often in their sleep, or from behind. Sometimes, new boyfriends or other family members carry out these acts of violence.

Psychological Violence

Psychological abuse can take the form of emotional abuse. This can include undermining the victims self-confidence, name-calling, implying mental illness and humiliation. Psychological abuse can also take the form of coercion and threats such as threatening to hurt, leave or report to welfare and health authorities. The female can also use the children forcing them to take sides in parental disputes and damaging father-child relationships by applying for sole custody and denying access. The partner might threaten to take the children away or threaten to injure the children unless their partner complies with their demands.

Controlling contact with friends and family can also inflict psychological abuse, preventing access to help and support. Many partners deny abuse and shift the responsibility for abuse onto the other partner. They blame alcohol/drugs/work pressure for their abusive behaviour. Men are sometimes forced to work two-jobs/long hours because of their partner's uncontrollable spending forcing the family into debt.

False Allegations

Men are often threatened with false allegations and in many cases these threats are followed through.

"The facts have become irrelevant. Everyone knows that restraining orders are granted to virtually all that apply. In many divorce cases, allegations of abuse are now used for tactical advantage. It has become essentially impossible to effectively represent a man against whom an allegation of domestic violence has been made".
Elaine Epstein, President, Massachusetts Bar Association.

False allegations are now being used increasingly as a tactic in separation or divorce. The Domestic Violence Act may have been intended as an instrument of protection but it is often used as a weapon of abuse. At a Women's Aid conference in Dublin Castle in April 1999 Judge Peter Smithwick, President of the District Court made reference to the fact that judges must be on their guard against false and exaggerated allegations.

Reasons for increased female violence towards males.

47

The psychologist John Archer in a study noted that, among female college students, twenty-nine percent admitted initiating an assault on a male partner. Of those women, half said they had no fear of retaliation or, since men could easily defend themselves, they did not see their own physical aggression as a problem. In other words, far from assuming that men are violent, women take men's non-aggression for granted.

He also suggests that as women have become independent of men, they have also become more violent towards them - because men have become dispensable. [1]

To illustrate how men have become dispensable, one simply has to observe the position of the male in the family unit. Fathers have turned into an optional extra. Instead of being seen as an integral part of the family unit, men are now permitted merely to bring - in certain circumstances defined by women - additional value to it.

"The steady growth of one-parent families – more than 1 in 10 of all Irish families in 1996 – and almost 9 in 10 headed by women – is evidence of the declining role of fatherhood."
Irish Independent, October 19th 1998

The very term "single-parent family" implies that there has been no loss but that this is a type of family complete in itself. It redefines the family as a unit without a man. Studies suggest a large number of children lose contact with their father's altogether following marital breakdown, with one third of children losing touch with one parent immediately after separation and another third losing touch five years after their parents' divorce.[2]

---

[1] Archer (2004).
[2] Phillips (1999).

There is an increasing trend for women to use men deliberately and instrumentally as the means to have a baby, but with no intention of living with the father as a family. Other women are doing without an identifiable father at all, reducing paternity to an emission in a test tube and dehumanising altogether the men who are used.

Effects of violence on men

Violence is damaging in a number of ways. The victim's physical and mental health is negatively impacted upon. There is ample evidence to demonstrate that victims of domestic abuse suffer grave damage to their self-esteem. Domestic violence also contributes to alcohol and drug abuse, mental illness, depression, suicide and para-suicide.[1] Because of the circumstances in which they depart their homes male victims often have nowhere to go. Statistics show that eighty-seven percent of those sleeping rough on the streets are men.[2]

It is standard practice in separation/divorce cases that women get the children, the family home and most of the family finances. Men are often evicted from their homes without just reason, marginalised in their children's lives and, in many cases, left living in comparative poverty.

These men continue to pay the mortgage and other expenses for the family home while still trying to provide accommodation for themselves. They are effectively stripped of their dignity, with their self-esteem shattered and are often depressed and suicidal. The victories and defeats in the judicial system are not marginal or partial, they are extreme. Men are conditioned to accept that they will lose everything simply because they are men.

---

[1] Cleary (2004).
[2] Department of the Enviornment et al (2003).

Men's reaction to violence

Men stay in abusive relationships because of the children, lack of alternative accommodation and often they still love the abuser and hope that things will change.

As Sabo & Gordon (1995) put it: 'Real men don't get sick, and when they do they don't complain about it and they don't seek help until their entire system begins to shut down.'

From an early age, boys are told that they are not supposed to cry and that they have to 'be strong soldiers'.[1]

In modern society, men are taking on increasingly more responsibilities. To handle this extra burden, it seems that men have had to prioritise certain things. While it is clear that men put caring and providing for their family at the top of their list, men have failed to take responsibility for their own health and well being. In the hierarchy of need, it would appear that men's own health needs are regularly displaced by the requirements of others.

Still others, when forced to recognise their symptoms, often deny or underplay them for fear of being seen as vulnerable and weak. While women have been socialised through history to express their emotions and depend on others, men have been told to be strong and self-reliant.

Recently the author observed a sign on display in the GP's surgery and it appears to be commonplace in most surgeries. It says 'It's a crime to hit a woman'. There is no disputing this fact but it failed to mention that it's also a crime to hit a

---

[1] Sabo & Gordon (1995).

man.

In a study by the North Eastern Health Board 2001 male victims of domestic violence had mixed views regarding their GPs' ability to help them in their hours of need. In general, it varied from 'ignorance' on the part of the GP, to a recognition that GPs are not equipped to deal with what, for many, is a new social phenomenon. The majority of men surveyed also reported that it was female doctors or practice nurses that were more sympathetic to male victims of domestic violence when they did seek help.

While men may wish to send out warning signals, they are prohibited from doing so due to an in-built belief that they have no right to ask others to rescue them from a plight that is, they believe, of their own making. They also know that admission of some failure can, in reality, lead to more failure, loss of promotion, loss of face among peers and family – and so they 'tough it out' in silence.

Little is known about the needs of men who are victims of domestic violence. These groups of men tend to suffer in silence and are ostracised by a society that still refuses to accept that women too can be perpetrators of violence. [1]

There is a need for male refuges, which currently are non-existent in Ireland. For many, being denied access to their own homes means taking refuge in, as men have revealed, cars, outhouses and their mothers' houses. These men are vulnerable, in need of help, support and a safe place. If society ignores one kind of violence, and implicitly maintains that it should be ignored, other kinds of violence become more acceptable. As Farrell (1994) put it 'When only one sex wins, both sexes lose.'

---

[1] Stakelum and Boland (2001)

In addition to male refuges initiatives like AMEN, the national support group for male victims of domestic violence must be supported so that they can reach a wider cohort of men than is currently the case.

Male victims fail to tell any family members of the situation and make excuses for their injuries even when they attend the hospital or the doctor. They fear the humiliation and stigma of disclosure even when the abuse is life threatening.

Society's reaction to violence against males

The training of the gardai and the legal system does not address the issue of male victims.
In one court case the judge commented to a soldier, *"do you expect me to believe that you, a defender of the nation, would allow this small woman to abuse you."*

It is society's expectations regarding the stereotypical male sex role, which most seriously affects men's ability to seek and obtain timely health care.

The male sex role stereotype demands that men be healthy, strong and self-sufficient. Often in an attempt to maintain a self-image consistent with society's expectations to be manly, men become reluctant, not just to admit, but often to recognise, their health needs. [1]

According to Stakelum and Boland men also faced many difficulties with social workers. This was as a result of a female bias that permeates current social work. Many men felt that, at best, they were not listened to and that, at worst, their stories were not taken seriously.

---

[1] Cleary (2004)

Social workers are mostly female, their client base is also predominantly female, and contact with men, when it does occur, is often secondary, following initial interaction with the female. This has meant that: The Social Services system has spent the last twenty years developing and refining decoding filters to decipher communications with a client base that has traditionally been female. Logically the decoding filters have been optimised to respond to women's experiences and are sensitive to female modes of expression. However this filter performs poorly when decoding male expression.[1]

There are now dozens of studies, which show that women are as violent towards their partners, if not more so, than men. Unlike most feminist research, these studies ask men as well as women whether they have ever been on the receiving end of violence from their partners.

They are therefore not only more balanced than studies which only ask about violence against women, but are more reliable indicators than official statistics which can be distorted by factors affecting the reporting rate - women using claims of violence as a weapon in custody cases, for example, or men who are too ashamed or embarrassed to reveal they have been abused.

A 1994 British study by Michelle Carrado and others interviewed eighteen hundred men and women with heterosexual partners. Some eleven percent of the men but only five percent of the women said their current partner had committed acts of violence towards them, ranging from pushing, through hitting, to stabbing. Five per cent of married or cohabiting men reported two or more acts of violence against them in a current relationship, compared

---

[1] Stakelum and Boland (2001)

with only one percent of women. A further ten percent of men but eleven percent of women said they had committed one of these violent acts. [2]

Study after study shows women are not merely violent in self-defence but strike the first blow in about half of all disputes. The American social scientists Murray Straus and Richard Gelles reported from two large national surveys that husbands and wives had assaulted each other at approximately equal rates, with women engaging in minor acts of violence more frequently. Elsewhere, they found more wives than husbands were severely violent towards their spouses. Moreover, there is now considerable evidence that women initiate severe violence more frequently than men. [1]

A survey of 1,037 young adults born between 1972 and 1973 in Dunedin, New Zealand, found that 18.6% of young women said they had perpetrated severe physical violence against their partners, compared with 5.7% of young men. Three times more women than men said they had kicked or bitten their partners, or hit them with their fists or with an object. [2]

The evidence about lesbians demolishes the idea that women are never the instigators of violence. According to Claire Renzetti, sociologist, violence in lesbian relationships occurs with about the same frequency as in heterosexual relationships. Lesbian batterers "display a terrifying ingenuity in their selection of abusive tactics, frequently tailoring the abuse to the specific vulnerabilities of their partners". Such abuse can be extremely violent, with women bitten, kicked, punched, thrown down stairs, and assaulted with weapons including guns, knives, whips and broken bottles. [3]

---

[2] Phillips (1999).
[1] Strauss & Gelles (1986).
[2] Phillips (1999).
[3] Renzetti (1991).

In law, a male victim faces two obstacles; firstly to prove he is a victim, and secondly, to ensure that his children are protected and do not become the new victims. Men very often remain in an abusive relationship for the sake and protection of their children.

Most men react by staying silent. Often this silence is encouraged by factors such as fear of ridicule and, the realisation that it is unlikely his partner will be evicted. Even when a man has proved he is the victim it seems his only course of action is to leave the home. He is then separated from his children and often experiences difficulty in obtaining realistic and regular contact with them. He is in fact treated as the perpetrator rather than the victim.

Modern medicine is aware of certain conditions, which may cause people to be violent, but we expect such sufferers to seek help or medical treatment. Men are expected to take responsibility for violence and abuse but no excuses are accepted. Yet when a female is violent society provides a list of excuses: Post-natal depression, stress, PMT, eating disorders, personality disorders, menopause, addictions, childhood traumas, provocation and self-defence. Although most men will be sensitive to these problems, they should not have to suffer violence as a consequence.

When a woman is violent and abusive in a relationship, it is not necessarily assumed that she is a bad mother. If a man is violent towards his partner, it is automatically assumed that he is an unfit parent. The law presumes that the children are almost always better off with their mother. Consequently the only options for men appear to put up with the abuse or to leave the home, since under the law there is no real protection for them.

If men attempt to report incidents of abuse they are met with blatant discrimination, disbelief and gender bias.

Society seems to want these men to go away because there is no simple solution to their plight and there are no support systems in place to deal with them.

Male Violence

This chapter highlights the social phenomena of female violence against men but it must not be overlooked that the majority of perpetrators of violence against men are male. In Northern Ireland 1,551 men were convicted of violence against the person in 2002 compared with 148 females. In the Republic of Ireland the total number of convictions for male offenders of acts of violence is eight times the corresponding female rate.[1]

Men are more likely to be violent towards fellow men than women.[2] In 2001 there were 2,374 male victims of assault compared to 740 females.[3] Men's fascination and respect for violence is often tied up with proving their manhood which, in part, explains their greater risk of being perpetrators or victims of homicide than females.[4] In 2000 there were thirty-nine victims of murder of which twenty-nine were men. In 2001 there were fifty-two murders in the republic of Ireland

[1] Garda Siochana (1999).
[2] Farrell (1986).
[3] Garda Siochana (2001).
[4] Stillion (1995).

of which thirty-nine were men. [5]

Society feels horror when innocent women and children are killed yet when men are killed they are described by the media as soldiers, miners, workers, people and often just numbers. Society is less horrified by the loss of male life because men are expected to play life-threatening roles. As a result of these expectations violence against men is not treated with the same condemnation as violence against females. Violence in any shape or form against either gender should not be tolerated.

Summary

There is now irrefutable evidence that women and men can be both perpetrators and victims of domestic violence. The only three gender neutral studies of domestic violence in the Republic of Ireland, carried out for Marriage and Relationship Counselling Service (MRCS 2001), ACCORD (2003) and the Department of Health (2003), have found that men and women abuse each other in roughly equal numbers.

These findings concur with results from all other two-sex studies and surveys carried out in the UK, Canada and the USA. Studies that portray men as predominantly perpetrators are not independent, neutral, balanced two-sex studies. They are predicated on the assumption that men are the aggressors and women the victims and are based on interviews with women only.

Violence is not only a male problem, but also a human one. Society will never solve the problem if it does not correctly identify it. It is true that men commit most recorded crime. It does not follow, however, that most men commit crime. Both

---

[5] Garda Crime Statistics (2001).

women and men are capable of aggression and violence, and violent men, like violent women, are not typical of their sex.

If a male victim seeks help, society should offer the same protection and help to him and his children as is given to female victims. Women should be judged by the same standards as men, and women who are violent should be held legally responsible for their actions.

Male Victims come from all walks of life, social backgrounds and cultures. They suffer society's stigma for not protecting themselves. They are victimised because they fail to conform to the male stereotype. They are disbelieved because they are men and are refused the status of victim. As a result they become depressed in their isolation, feel suicidal and sometimes take their own lives without disclosure. The following chapter will discuss suicide in men and will offer possible theories as to why eighty percent of suicides are male.

Chapter Four

Suicide

Introduction:

The following chapter will discuss suicide in Ireland and more specifically suicide in Irish men. The chapter will review the statistics available and offer suggestions as to why eighty percent of suicides are male.

Suicide Statistics.

Every week, eight people in the Republic of Ireland will successfully take their own lives and another one hundred will attempt suicide. In Ireland, there are around four hundred and fifty suicide deaths each year. This figure represents around 1.5% of all deaths in Ireland annually. More people die by suicide each year than in road accidents.

In 2002 there were four hundred and fifty-one suicides registered by the Central Statistics Office compared with two hundred and forty-nine vehicle accident deaths.[1] Figures show that between 1988 and 1999 the suicide rate in Ireland increased by ninety percent. In 1999 there were four hundred and thirty-nine suicides in total, almost eighty percent of which were male. Suicide among young men in this country continues to rise dramatically and they choose more violent means of suicide than females.[2]

The increasing suicide trend, both internationally and in

---

[1] Chambers (2003).
[2] CSO (2001).

Ireland is now a major health problem. This is particularly so for young Irish men, where there has been a four fold increase in the suicide rate since 1990. The rate of suicide among young males is more than six times as high as among young females.[1]

Between 1945 and 1995 the rate of suicide in Ireland rose from 2.38 per 100,000 populations to 10.69 per 100,000. The increase in suicide in recent decades however has been primarily a male phenomenon.

In the preparation of the Interim Report of the National Task Force on suicide it was found that suicide is the most common cause of death among fifteen to twenty-four year old males in the Republic of Ireland, and is equal to a rate of 19.5 per 100,000 population compared with 2.1 per 100,000 among fifteen to twenty-four year old women.[2]

During the period from 1991 to 1993 young male suicide deaths increased from a position where they were as frequent as cancer deaths in 1976 to greatly exceeding cancer deaths by 1993. The overall rate of suicide among men in 1995 was 17.2 per 100,000 population compared with a rate of 4.3 among women. In recent years, four to five times more men than women died by suicide in Ireland.[3]

In most countries that return data to the WHO, the suicide rate increases with age. In Ireland, the rate of suicide peaks among young men. Suicide rates are highest among young men in their twenties. [4]

In 1998, the Republic of Ireland ranked sixth amongst fellow

---

[1] CSO (2001).
[2] Department of Health and Children 1998b
[3] CSO 2002a, NISRA (2002).
[4] Chambers (2003).

EU countries in terms of standardised rates amongst men due to suicide and intentional self-harm (22.8 per 100,000). Finland ranked the highest with a rate of 36.8 per 100,0000 and Greece the lowest with a rate of 5.7 per 100,000.[1]

According to the report of the National Suicide Review Group (2001), almost half of all suicides in the Republic of Ireland are by hanging (49.7%). For males, hanging accounted for more than half of all suicides with drowning and poisoning accounting for 17.7% and 14.2% respectively. Suicide by firearms is less common for males overall, but accounts for one in eight young males who died from suicide (15-24 years) and almost as many in elderly men (11.3% over 64 year olds).

Stillion (1995) notes that often males select more violent methods compared with females. Stillion suggests men see surviving a suicide attempt as a mark against their masculine adequacy. Canettos' research found that traditional masculine expectations elevated the likelihood of a suicide resulting in a fatal outcome for some men.[2]

Figures underestimate the true suicide rate in that in most countries it is under reported. The under reporting arises because there is no commonly accepted definition of suicide for data collection purposes. There are legal restrictions on coroners in the latitude given to them in declaring a suicide death.

A certain proportion of fatal road traffic accidents and poisonings, which are in fact suicides will not be reported as such, because of lack of evidence. Finally there is an understandable tendency of bereaved families, friends and the medical profession to conceal suicide deaths.

---

[1] Eurostat (2000).
[2] Canettos (1995).

The extent of under reporting has varied between countries, with studies reporting a two to fourfold underestimate. In Ireland there was significant under reporting, as evidenced by the high number of deaths reported as being of "undetermined cause". In recent times there has been a dramatic improvement, as reflected by the drop in deaths of "undetermined cause" from one hundred and nineteen in 1971 to nine in 1995. However, it does seem likely that some deaths classified as "undetermined" or "accidental" are suicide deaths.[1]

Reasons for suicide:

Studies have shown that countries that have an increasing suicide rate in young people are also going through significant social change.[2]

The rate of suicidal behaviours have also been reported to have increased significantly among post-pubertal adolescent males attending the psychiatric services in the past twenty years and this has been found to be explained by increasing alcohol misuse.[3]

Suicide deaths can be best explained by an interaction of three factors, namely psychiatric illness, usually in the form of depression, losses in life, such as bereavement, marital breakdown, unemployment, exam or work failure and alcohol or illicit drug abuse. For example, in a young male suicide victim use of illicit drugs is often cited as the cause of suicide.[4]

---

[1] Barraclough et al (1974).
[2] Aware (1999).
[3] Fombonne (1998).
[4] Aware (1999)

Suicide rates are generally lowest in women, married individuals and those in the higher socio-economic groups. There is a clear statistical association between unemployment and suicide, especially in men.[1]

Mental Illness

There is a highly consistent association between mental illness and suicide, with over ninety percent of suicide victims being diagnosed as mentally ill.[2] Forty to seventy per cent are found to have a mood disorder, fifteen to twenty-five percent alcoholism, with drug abuse exceeding affective disorder in young people. Studies show that between twenty-six and fifty-three percent of adolescent suicide victims abused alcohol and nine to seventeen percent habitually abused some other drug.[3]

Studies have found that depression was highest in sixteen to twenty-two year olds from divorced families who had low self-esteem at sixteen and lacked an intimate relationship in young adulthood.[4]

Other types of environmental factors that are associated with depression in this age group are physical or sexual abuse, loss of a parent, sibling or close friend and being homosexual.[5]

Suicide is more likely to occur at the start and at the end of the depressive episode, and, at a societal level, at the beginning and end of the winter months.

Physical Illness

---

[1] Platt et al (1984)
[2] Department of Health (1996).
[3] Martunnen et al (1991).
[4] Rey (1995).
[5] Feldman & Wilson (1997).

Chronic physical disorders are relatively common among suicide victims, particularly elderly males. Cancers, diseases of the central nervous system, peptic ulcer disease, genital-urinary disorders and epilepsy are frequently cited.[1] The link between suicide and physical illness may be due to several factors including pain, depression, alcohol abuse and difficulty coming to terms with the handicap of a debilitating or terminal illness.[2]

Family History of Suicide and Biochemical Abnormalities

Some studies show that suicidal behaviour appears to cluster in families,[3] and the risk of suicide appears to be increased in the biological relatives of adoptees who have committed suicide.[4] This raises the possibility of a genetic predisposition, implicating some biochemical brain abnormality. One such possibility is the neurotransmitter serotonin, whose breakdown products have been found to be lower in depressives with suicidal behaviour.

Why Men kill themselves.

The above reasons are often used to explain suicide but they fail to explain why six times more young men kill themselves than women, the following paragraphs will offer possible suggestions for this.

The Woman's Movement.

---

[1] Roy (1983).
[2] Barraclough et al (1974).
[3] Tsuang (1983).
[4] Schulsinger et al (1979).

The women's movement has done more than question the role of women – it reinforces the notion that women had rights to what was the traditional male role. Nothing tells men that they have rights to what was the traditional female role, that is, the rights to stay at home full or part-time while the wife or partner supports him.[1]

The influx of women into the workforce, rather than easing the burden of responsibility for men, has only served to heighten the ambiguity of their role. This has left some men feeling devalued and undermined. The ability to work is still the defining health benchmark for many men. Emotional health, in contrast, is still given far less priority.

When a man loses his status in the public domain of work he is not equipped to deal with the loss of self. Men's emotional qualities have not been sufficiently nurtured to allow men to value themselves outside the context of work. Failure in this domain could lead, not only to emotional turmoil, but also on occasion, to suicide.[2]

Traditionally, men have defined their lives, their identities, and the very essence of their masculinity, in terms of work. They have prided themselves in the work that only they could do. With increasingly more women sharing the role of provider, men no longer have work as a yardstick with which to measure their own unique self worth.

Inability to express emotions or look for help.

Parental death during childhood may increase the risk of suicide in adulthood and there is evidence that it is strongly

---

[1] Farrell (1993).
[2] Stakelum & Boland (2001).

linked to suicide attempts.[3] Being recently bereaved is also a suicide risk factor.[4] Recent loss such as the break-up of a sexual relationship, particularly in young males, is another substantial risk factor.[1]

Studies of the impact of the Samaritans have failed to show that they make a significant impact on suicide rates. Only four percent of suicide victims ever make contact with the Samaritans and four percent of those attempting suicide make contact in the week prior to the attempt.[2]

The consensus seems to be that suicide hotlines are minimally effective in reducing suicidal behaviour and where they have produced some reduction it is among young women, who are the most frequent users of these services.[3]

Men with depression are less likely to be in contact with the health services, and when they are, they present with depression in an atypical manner.

The results of two Irish studies reinforce the finding that men with depression do not tend to seek help. A national study of public attitudes to depression in Ireland revealed that young men were significantly more likely than women and men of an older age group to regard those with depression as "feeling sorry for themselves" and tended to be dismissive of losses such as bereavement as a cause of depression.[4]

A second study, which focused on the attitudes to the management of depression in general practice, showed that

---

[3] Roy (1983).
[4] Barraclough et al (1974).
[1] Aware (1999).
[2] Barraclough & Shea (1972).
[3] Shaffer et al (1995).
[4] McKeown & Carrick (1991).

young men were significantly less willing to attend their general practitioners for treatment of psychological conditions.[5]

While men may wish to send out warning signals, they are prohibited from doing so due to an in-built belief that they have no right to ask others to rescue them from a plight that is, they believe, of their own making. They also know that admission of some failure can, in reality, lead to more failure, loss of promotion, loss of face among peers and family – and so they 'tough it out' in silence.

Men's own unwillingness to seek help contributes to the social construction of their invulnerability to depression.[1]

In response to depression, men are more likely than women to rely on themselves, to withdraw socially or to talk themselves out of depression.[2]

Parents teach male infants to perform rather than cry by picking up the males less frequently than the female infant when he cries. By the age of thirteen months, boys who are picked up less are already more likely to "tough it out" and refrain from crying. By the time the boy subliminally absorbs the purpose of these messages, he is already more comfortable with behaviour such as solving his own problems or "doing" rather than complaining or crying.[3]

In an experimental setting, the Condreys asked observers to comment on the feelings expressed by a nine-month old infant. If the observers were told the infant was a boy, they

---

[5] Gavigan & McKeown (1995).
[1] Courtenay 2000).
[2] Warren (1983).
[3] Goldberg & Lewis (1969).

labelled the crying "anger." If they were told it was a girl, they labelled the exact same crying by the same child at the same time "fear".[4]

When men do express feelings, as in the Condrey experiment, society tends to find ways of reinforcing our view of men as insensitive, unfeeling beings.

Identification with traditional masculinity has been linked to the act of taking one's life amongst males.[1]

Discrimination against men: The single Father.

The common experience of fathers seeking custody of their children has been one of frustration, anger, and disbelief with the current legal system. These emotions are the result of a system that does not honour the notion of equality for all parties in the custody battle, but rather, acts on the premise that mothers are the most suitable custodians for children until proven otherwise.[2]

This bias often manifests itself in sole custody orders in favour of the mother and restricted access and alienation of fathers. Failure to give fathers equal and unbiased rights to the custody of their children will undoubtedly have serious health consequences for this group of men.

The Men's Council of Ireland has claimed that separated fathers were being driven to desperate actions, including abduction and the taking of their own lives. The Council has called for an urgent overhaul of the family law system, which they say, is adversarial. In marital breakdown, men are the biggest losers, losing their homes, children and most of their

---

[4] Condrey (1976).
[1] Sabo 1999).
[2] Stakelum & Boland (2001).

income.

In a study of men conducted by the North Eastern Health board in 2001 other issues at a societal level also emerged as barriers to active fatherhood. Men interviewed in the study referred, in particular, to recent revelations of child sexual abuse and to how these have negatively impacted upon the natural intimacy of the father-child relationship. This is particularly true of fathers who are victims of domestic violence, or who are in the process of striving for custody of their children.[1] Fathers appear to have an ever-constant threat of being falsely accused of abusing their own children.

In situations of marital separation, men not only have to cope with loss of involvement in their children's lives but must also deal with institutions, like health boards, the Gardaí and the judicial system, which continue to support the traditional notion that women are the primary caregivers of children. The legitimacy of motherhood is never in doubt, yet men have to fight their case through the judicial system to gain equal rights of access.

As with women, men experience emotional rejection when they separate but they, unlike women, are much more likely to be involuntarily deprived of their children, thus experiencing a double dose of emotional rejection.

Supports should be put in place for fathers who don't get to see their children. The statutory services should provide guidance and practical help to these men bearing in mind the negative emotional impact of being alienated from the family unit.

---

[1] Stakelum & Boland (2001).

69

Failure of the Health System

Social structures reinforce the ethos of self-care among women by making medical centres more attractive to women. They also raise awareness among women of the need to maintain and care for their health through 'Well Woman' clinics.

The majority of surgeries have well woman clinics but there are very few doctors that would have a man's clinic so as to make men aware of their health.

Health promotion initiatives targeted at women, at different stages of the life cycle, have been established for some time. Similar approaches should also be considered for men.

In addition to socio-cultural barriers, there are also institutional barriers to help seeking. These are inflexible surgery times, the feminisation of doctors' waiting rooms and protracted waiting times.

Inflexible surgery times affect men, in particular, those who work in occupations like farming or the construction industry, where inflexible working arrangements compete with inflexible surgery times.

GP surgeries are often deemed by men to be places where females, not males, congregate. If one examines surgeries, even down to something very basic such as the available reading material in the waiting area, the majority of literature appears to be magazines specifically for women. This contributes in creating the perception that the service is predominantly for females.

Young people, particularly men, who commit suicide are less likely to have been in contact with the psychiatric services and may be less open emotionally. Aware (1999). The system fails these men in not providing them with appropriate, adequate and effective support.

An Investigation of One Hundred Suicides (Kelleher et al.2000) show males who died from suicide were significantly younger than female suicides. Among those aged between fifteen and forty-four years old, males outnumbered females by four to one. After the age of forty-five years, the number of men and women is almost equal. The numbers treated for psychiatric illness by a general practitioner or psychiatrist prior to death also shows major divergence between the sexes. Over eighty per-cent of the women were known to have been medically treated, as opposed to forty-nine per-cent of the men.

Men do not seek help in the way women do. Society must encourage men to seek help.

Alienated by society.

Society tells young women on the verge of adulthood that they are by nature sensitive, caring, humane and compassionate, it tells its male young that they will grow up to be insensitive brutes, unworthy of sympathy or respect.

Young women are now offered multiple lifestyle choices between career and motherhood, workplace and home. Young men are told that they must make way for their hitherto disadvantaged sisters. Young men are told they must remain strong unless otherwise indicated.

This reality is reflected in the figures for both suicide and what is called "attempted suicide". Many more women than men actually attempt suicide, but many more men "succeed". The National Para-suicide Registry recorded 4,788 female cases in 2002 compared with 3,513 male cases recorded in the same period.

In truth, they are two quite distinct phenomena: attempted

suicide is a cry for help that almost certainly anticipates the relief of compassion; suicide is that act of someone who expects no help. In general, it is women who threaten to kill themselves and men who kill themselves.

One of the traditional excuses about suicide has been that it is the consequence of mental illness. The purpose of emphasising this connection has been to spare the families of suicide victims, but also society at large, from the guilt arising from the accusation that a suicide might otherwise represent.

For a long time, it has been a central psychiatric belief that women have a greater tendency towards depression than men, yet many fewer women end up killing themselves. This suggests that suicide has much less to do with depression and more as a result of external and environmental factors including society and attitudes to the depressed person.

One of the reasons why men lose hope is because society itself downplays, distorts, or even ignores the problem.

Suicide Prevention

In 1998 Ireland's National Task Force on Suicide report made wide ranging recommendations, but without setting measurable targets.[1]

The Finnish strategy is particularly comprehensive and is well developed. It is the only national strategy that has a conceptual framework with a clear definition of suicide prevention. Its prevention strategy is at several levels: tertiary prevention which focuses on those who have

---

[1] Department of Health and Children (1998).

attempted or planned suicide and the method they use, secondary prevention attempts to eliminate or reduce conditions such as mental illness, intoxicant problems, physical illness and life crises, which under certain circumstances can lead to suicide, and primary prevention which aims to enhance every individual's inner resources and living conditions.

One of the strengths of the Finnish approach is the development of local initiative and commitment. It sets out clearly what each agency is expected to do.

Given the increasing suicide rate in young men, Finland has targeted this group for special attention. In addition to their use of a comprehensive range of measures, they emphasise the need to build self-esteem, diminish the sense of alienation, and they are considering the usefulness of public service duty as a means of aiding personal development.

They also believe that young people wishing to become independent from their families should be prepared for and assisted in doing so. They emphasise the need to take any self-destructive behaviour seriously in young people and a guidebook on support and help for young people is made available to the general public by specialists.

There is some suggestion that the comprehensive range of suicide prevention measures in Finland have resulted in a 16% reduction in the rate of violent suicide deaths which usually occur in men, since 1990.[1]

In Ireland suicide rates are highest among young men in their twenties and prevention efforts must be targeted accordingly. Suicide prevention and research should have a

---

[1] Hakko et al (1998).

gendered focus since the epidemiology of suicide differs significantly between the genders. Prevention should focus on men between eighteen and thirty-four years as they account for forty percent of all suicides in Ireland each year.[2]

Consideration should be given to the preferences of young men when developing suicide bereavement support services. Many of these services have been developed with a strong pastoral and sometimes spiritual or religious theme. This approach may not be appropriate for young men who are increasingly likely to be atheist (over 200,000 people categorised as 'No Religion" or 'Not stated' in 2002 Census).

Summary

There are still significant gaps in society's understanding of suicide; why it occurs and how it can best be prevented. There is a danger that society will grow less sensitive to personal despair and come to regard suicide as a normal, or relatively acceptable, method of solving personal crisis.

Since actual suicide predominantly affects men, suicide prevention programs need to be male-specific, and address the underlying social and psychological causes that affect men. This common sense principle is used in designing female-specific programs on osteoporosis, eating disorders, and breast cancer.

The health services need to come to young men rather than vice versa. It is vital that mental health and health promotion and education occur at a young age. Young males should be encouraged to access support from family and friends. There is a need for more general information being available on

---

[2] Chambers (2003).

mental health issues and support services.

There needs to be an increase in the efforts to reduce suicide rates in young men. Efforts have to be made to improve self-esteem, reduce alienation and promote problem-solving approach to life crises in young males. Prompt treatment of suicide attempts must be encouraged and all destructive behaviour taken seriously.

Given the increase in suicide rate in young men, the level of alienation in this group needs to be studied and appropriate interventions effected. The promotion of men's emotional health requires a broad partnership beyond the mental health services. Educational services and primary healthcare services must address the emotional needs of men.

The concluding chapter will summarise the previous chapters and offer suggestions and recommendations as to what can be done to improve not only the life expectancy but also the quality of men's lives.

Chapter Five

Promoting Men's Health Conclusions and Recommendations

Although research is limited in Ireland, it is well documented internationally that compared to women, men have limited contacts with physicians and healthcare services in general.[1] Hence it is hardly surprising to learn that for almost every condition common to both sexes the outcome for men tends to be poorer.

In terms of accessing health service, men are slower to notice signs of illness, and when they do, they are less likely to consult their doctor.[2] It has been estimated that forty percent of male consultations are at the prompting of a female. Eight out of ten men admit to waiting too long before going to see their doctor.[3]

Men have a lack of awareness as to when they should attend for screening. There is an absence of preventative healthcare ethos in the current delivery of general practice. Men unlike women are not socialised into the health culture from an early age, and are therefore less likely to develop the confidence to seek preventative help. Men are less likely to interpret their symptoms as arising from physical symptoms, which may be a form of denial.[4]

---

[1] Courtenay (1998).
[2] Kraemer (2000).
[3] Denyer (1998).
[4] Stakelum & Boland (2001).

Irish men's lack of knowledge of fundamental health issues is evidence that health has never been on the agenda for many Irish men. In a study by Richardson (2004) less than half the respondents knew what the function of the prostate gland was while almost one in four men were unable to correctly identify its location. Between a third and a half of respondents were not aware of the most common prostate cancer symptoms.

Three out of four men aged between eighteen and twenty-nine years were not aware that young men were at highest risk of developing testicular cancer, with almost half of the same age category never having heard of testicular self examination.[1]

With the exception of O' Dowd et al (1998) and more recently Clarke (2000), Irish research into male health issues is most noted by its absence. While women it seems have taken measures to ensure that health issues have shifted from the realm of ideology to social policy the same cannot be said of men's health.

International studies show that, from birth until the age of five, boys attend their general practitioner more frequently than girls. Between five and fourteen years there is little difference between the sexes in terms of GP attendance. From fourteen years old, however, when sex roles become established, men become less frequent GP attendees. This reluctance to seek help seems to reach a peak in middle age.[2] In addition, Cook et al. (1990) found that in all social classes, ten percent of men aged between forty-six and sixty-five years did not consult their GP over a three year period, and a further forty-four percent consulted, on average, twice a year or less.

---

[1] Richardson (2004).
[2] Wilson (1998).

Late presentation can result in poor health outcomes, and explains why men, despite being half as likely as women to develop malignant melanoma, are twice as likely to die.[1]

It was not until very recently that men have been identified as a target population for the strategic planning of healthcare in the Republic of Ireland (Department of Health and Children 2001). However as Richardson (2003) notes, there still remains a fundamental lack of understanding and clarity about what is meant by 'men's health' in Ireland.

Men in Ireland die, on average, nearly six years younger than women do, and have higher death rates at all ages, and for all leading causes of death. Evidence of sex differences in the incidence, symptoms and prognosis of a wide range of health problems is also well documented. There has, however, been little evidence to date that these differences are reflected in the planning and delivery of healthcare, or in wider social and economic policies.[2]

Irish men have the fifth lowest life expectancy at birth, and this falls to the lowest life expectancy at age sixty-five years (13.9 years, EU average 15.0 years). Overall the findings, not just in Ireland but in the developed world, suggest that men have substantial health inferiority in terms of life expectancy.

Whilst the issue of women's health (Department of Health and Children 1997) has been the source of extensive consultation and careful strategic planning in the Republic of Ireland, the same cannot be said for men's health. Although men have been identified, as a target population for the first time, in the strategic planning of health promotion and

---

[1] Banks (2001).
[2] Doyal (2001).

healthcare (Department of Health and Children 2001) there appears to have been little momentum to date to act on these initiatives.

Male occupations, particularly the lower skilled and semiskilled variety, are by necessity, 'dirty' and 'hazardous' – a factor that women rarely have to contend with. Shift work, deep shaft mining and hard physical labour are often an integral part of these men's working lives and even if there are health and safety measures in place, the risks to their health during their working day will always be greater than those faced by women.

Men's health is under researched both clinically and in terms of health promotion. Men are 1.6 times as likely as women to die from one of the top ten causes of death. The National Institutes of Health, the federal focal point for medical research in the United States spends nearly four times as much on female-specific health research as on male-specific research. The Department of Health and Human Services' National Cancer Institute in the United States spends three and half times as much money on breast cancer research as on prostate cancer research. Prostate cancer makes up thirty-seven of all cancer cases but receives only five percent of federal research funding.[1]

The number and quality of government-funded women's health education projects is outstanding. Outreach programs teach women about breast cancer and cervical cancer. There are few if any programs, which educate men about their own gender-specific health needs. Men need education about the cancers, which disproportionately affect them, such as prostate cancer, skin cancer and colorectal cancer. Young men need education on testicular cancer. Most importantly,

---

[1] Sacks (2002).

men need to be encouraged to seek preventative health care.

One of the reasons for the neglect of promoting men's health initiatives is the common but nonetheless false perception that the government and the scientific community have paid more attention to men's health than to women's. In the US in 1990 Senator Barbara Mikulski made national headlines by citing the fact that women-specific health research comprised only fourteen percent of the budget of the National Institute of Health (NIH). She called it *"blatant discrimination"* and led the successful campaign for the creation of the Office of Women's Health. Mikulski and many in the media who publicized Mikulski's claims failed to realise that only 6.5% of the NIH's budget went to male-specific research and that the vast majority of the NIH's research was gender neutral.[1]

The myth of women's medical neglect has bred needless resentment in many women. It has also hampered efforts to improve health care for men, who are much less likely to get regular medical check-ups or to seek care promptly when they have symptoms of illness. Fears of short-changing women make it difficult for men's health programs to get funding.

Recent Men's health initiatives
A Conference on Men's Health was held in 1998. The first National Men's Health Conference was held in December 2004. Men's health workshops are being developed in community settings and on FÁS schemes.

Over the past number of years the Health Promotion Department of the South-Eastern Health Board began working on Men's Health. It set up a working group in 1999 to review the area of men's health and identify opportunities

---

[1] Sacks (2002).

for development.

The National Health Strategy calls for a policy on men's health and health promotion to be developed. The National Health Promotion Strategy 2000-2005 also identified the development of a national plan for men's health as an important initiative. The Department has funded the appointment of a Men's Health Research Officer in the South-Eastern Health Board.

Issues such as Irishmen's concept of health, their knowledge, beliefs and attitudes to health and illness, health behaviours and risk behaviours, and the barriers that Irishmen perceive in accessing the health services are being researched. The findings of this research will inform the development of the new men's health policy.

There have been some recent initiatives in men's health. November 2003 the Irish Cancer Society launched it's 'NCT' programme, which was the first national campaign directed at cancer awareness for men. The North Eastern Health Board produced a report on men's health in 2001 ('Men Talking'), and has since been proactive in developing a number of men's health initiatives within the North Eastern region.

Recommendations

- It would appear that currently, the majority of health-promotion information is bypassing men. This is primarily because it is neither targeted at, nor delivered, with men in mind. The little information that does exist is located in health centres – venues not often frequented by males. Even within these locations, it is the women's health agenda that seems to be given greater priority. An example of this is when one enters a doctor's surgery and one sees items on pregnancy, the menopause and other female specific issues yet nothing of male specific conditions.

- Men need to be targeted in locations where they meet and congregate. In addition to the workplace, sporting fixtures are ideal venues for the delivery of messages on men's health. Organisations such as, the GAA, local gun clubs, rugby and golf clubs, men's toilets and locker rooms are locations highly amenable to raising awareness of men's health issues. Large high profile events with a strong male viewership such as snooker championships, golfing championships, GAA and rugby events should all be used to reinforce messages delivered at national level.

- It is essential that a health-promoting ethos be created throughout the schooling cycle. There is a need for sport, fitness and physical education programmes to be taken seriously by schools. There should be equity across all schools with regard to time allotted to sporting activities and the subject should be taught by teachers qualified in the area. The emphasis should not just be on fitness but it should also include theory about health-related issues.

- Campaigns should target young men specifically. Newspaper features, television programs, widespread advertisement campaigns and local radio should be used as a medium of communication. A holistic approach to men's health at both a policy and health service delivery level that seeks to address the underlying causes of men's health issues needs to be adopted.

- There is a need for greater understanding and appreciation of why men take risks with their health, why they are more likely to engage in health damaging behaviours and why they are prone to present late during the course of an illness. By generating a better understanding of how men experience their health and illness we may be better able to target men more effectively.

- There needs to be an increased priority on men's health in the workplace that embraces the workplace as a key setting for delivering men's health initiatives and that involves both employers and representative bodies working in a cohesive way on promoting men's health.

- There needs to be an increase in the resources allocated to develop help lines and Internet sites as mediums of help seeking that are deemed to be attractive and acceptable to men. The availability of such supports also needs to be adequately publicised. Continued efforts are needed to raise the profile and level of acceptability of men's health issues, and to open up channels to services for men who require help. There is an urgent need to challenge the stigma that for some men continues to be associated with seeking help for depression.

- An increase in focus should be placed on more health promoting stress management initiatives for men, particularly in the workplace, and that more flexible and family friendly work practices are made available in particular to fathers of young children.

- There needs to be national male specific health promotion initiatives. Health promotion initiatives should take place at the level of general practice specially tailored to meet the changing health needs of men across the life cycle. A department of men's health should be established. This would involve the appointment of a Men's Health co-ordinator that would ensure that men's health issues are constantly kept in focus.

- It is vital that research increasingly takes 'sex differences' into account. Where the population analyzed includes men and women, the findings should be broken down by sex. This is as important as findings stratified by age, social class or ethnicity. A more critical appraisal of such sex differences (i.e. a 'gendered' approach to health) is called for in the future.

- Research clearly indicates that men and women engage in health differently, hence, training should be provided for health professionals and service providers on men's health issues and on working with men as a specific sub-group. Training is particularly needed on how to identify men's health needs at the local level and how to design and deliver effective services for men.

- There is an urgent need for more health promotion initiatives that are specifically targeted at men rather than based on the traditional population-wide approach.

- It is no longer sufficient to tell men that they need to be more open about their feelings, when the dominant discourse still informs them that they need to be macho and deal with their own problems.

- Changes need to be rooted in structural changes and buoyed by new male friendly institutional realities.

- National health campaigns raising the awareness of men and the general population, while worthwhile must be reinforced with a concerted effort by governments, academic departments, health research bodies to challenge current masculine ideologies.

- It is not just the impact of lifestyles and biology on health status but also society's expectations of men that also need to be addressed. Such expectations have created an environment in which men are less able than women to recognise physical and emotional distress and to seek help.

- There needs to be a recognition of men's health as an academic discipline in which more of the work being undertaken in different areas of medical and social sciences are tied together to give a deeper understanding of what impacts on the health of men.

- Studies are needed on how men can be supported to best cope with acute and chronic illness and how rehabilitation can be fashioned to enable men to manage their illnesses more effectively.

Summary

Future initiatives should focus not only on men's health in a narrow biomedical sense, but embrace initiatives that challenge the manner in which males are socialised.

In shaping health policies, the value of preventative medicine must be endorsed. Men need to be educated in order to come to grips with their own behaviour and to reach a real understanding of their basic health needs.

Women and men are not isolated from each other. When men die prematurely, the women who love them are affected as well. It is not the intention of this publication to play gender politics with medicine but to redirect energy and resources towards providing better care for everyone.

References:

1. Archer J., 'The trouble with 'doing boy'', The Psychologist, March 2004, Vol. 17 No 3.

2. Armstrong J (1999), Men's Health, The Common Sense Approach, Newleaf Publications, Dublin.

3. Aware, (1998), Suicide in Ireland, Aware Publications.

4. Balanda K, Wilde J. (2001) Inequalities in Mortality: A report on All-Ireland Mortality Data, The Institute of Public Health in Ireland, 6 Kildare Street, Dublin.

5. Banks I, (2001), No mans land: men, illness and the NHS, BMJ; 323.

6. Barraclough B, Bunch J, Nelson B, Sainsbury P (1974) A hundred cases of suicide: clinical aspects. British Journal of Psychiatry 125; 355-373.

7. Barraclough B, Shea M (1972) A comparison between Samaritan suicides and living Samaritan clients. British Journal of Psychiatry, 120; 79 - 84

8. Bulla A, (2003), Hidden Menace in Improving Our Defences Against the Hidden Cancer Killing Men, The Sunday Times, 20th April 2003.

9. Broverman IK, (1972). "Sex-Role Stereotypes: A current Appraisal". Journal of social issues 28:59-78.

10. Cahill E, (2002). The Irish Independent, Features, 7th February.

11. Canettos S, (1995), Men who survive a suicidal act, Men's Health and Illness: Gender, Power and the body, 46-67, Thousand Oaks, CA: Sage Publishing.

12. Central Statistics Office (2000a), Statistical Yearbook of Ireland: 2002, Information Section, Cork.

13. Central Statistics Office (2000b), Ireland North and South: A Statistical Profile: 2002, Information Section, Cork.

14. Central Statistics Office (2002a), Statistical Yearbook of Ireland: 2002, Information Section, Cork.

15. Chambers (2003), The Male Perspective, Young Men's Outlook on life. National Suicide Research Foundation.

16. Clarke, A. (2000) Masculinity in Crisis. Chatto & Windus, London.

17. Cleary 2004. Issues for male victims of domestic abuse, Amen Publications, Navan.

18. Condrey J, (1976). "Sex differences: A Study in the Eye of the beholder", Child Development, vol. 47, 1976 pp. 812-819.

19. Cook D.G., Morris J. K., Walker M., and Shaper A. G. (1990). Consultation rates among middle – aged men in general practice over three years. British Medical Journal 301, 647-50.

20. Courtenay W, (2000), Constructions of Masculinity and Their Influence on Men's Well-being, Social Science Medicine, 50(10): 1385-1401.

21. Courtenay WH, (1998), College Men's Health: An Overview and A Call to Action, Journal of American College Health, May 46(6): 279-90

22. Courtenay W, (2000), Constructions of Masculinity and Their Influence on Men's Well-being, Social Science Medicine, 50(10): 1385-1401.

23. Dearnaley DP, Huddart RA, Horwich A (2001) Managing testicular cancer. British Medical Journal Vol. 322:1583-1588

24. Deaux K, Wrightsman LS, (1984). Social Psychology in the 80's. Monterey, California, Brooks/Cole Publishing Company.

25. Deaux K, (1992). *"Sex Differences"* in Encyclopaedia of Sociology Ed. by E.F. Borgatta. New York, Macmillan, Toronto, Collier Macmillan Canada, New York, Maxwell Macmillan International.

26. Deaux K, (1984). From individual differences to social categories. Analysis of a decades research on gender. American Psychologist 105-115 Vol.39 No.2. Feb.

27. Deaux K, and Major B, (1987). Putting gender into context: An interactive model of gender-related behaviour. Psychological Review 94:369-389.

28. Denyer S. (1998) 'It's Dangerous to be a Man! The Health of men in the North West.' Presentation given at Men's Health Conference in Bundoran Donegal.

29. Department of Health and Children, (2002), Health Statistics 2002, Dublin, Stationery Office.

30. Department of Health (1996) National Task Force on Suicide: Interim Report. Dublin: Government Publications, 1996.

31. Department of Health and Children, (1998b), Interim Report of the National Task force on suicide, Dublin, Stationery Office.

32. Department of health (2002) Tackling health inequalities. The Department of Health, London

33. Department of Health and Children, (2002), Health Statistics 2002, Dublin, Stationery Office.

34. Department of Health and Children, (2001), Quality and Fairness; A Health System for you, Dublin, Stationery Office.

35. Department of Health and Children, (1997), A plan for women's health 1997-99, Dublin, Stationery Office.

36. Department of the Environment and Local Government and Simon Community, (2003)."Homelessness – An Integrated Strategy", Report May 2003.

37. Dowd (2002), Men's Health: Impact of Prostate-related Problems on Men in Work and Society, Department of Community Health and General Practice, Trinity College Dublin.

38. Doyal L, (2001), Sex, Gender and Health, The need

for a new approach, British Medical Journal Vol 323.

39. Eagly AE, (1987). Sex differences in social behaviour: A social role interpretation. Hillsdale, N.J., Erlbaum.

40. Eurostat (2002) The Life of men and women in Europe: a statistical portrait 1980 – 2000

41. Eurostat Yearbook (2002): The statistical guide to Europe, data 1990-2000

42. Eurostat (2002) The Life of Men and Women in Europe: A statistical portrait. Data 1980 – 2000, Luxembourg: Office for Official Publications of the European Communities.

43. Eurostat (2002) European Social Statistics: Demography, Luxembourg: Office for Official Publications of the European Communities, 2002

44. Eurostat (2002) The life of men and women in Europe, a statistical portrait 1980 – 2000.

45. Eurostat (2000), Key Data on Health.

46. Farrell W. (1993) The Myth of Male Power: Why men are the disposable Sex.4th Edition. Fourth Estate London.

47. Farrell W (1986). Why Men are the way they are. Mc Graw-Hill, New York.

48. Feldman M. and Wilson A. (1997) Adolescent suicidality in urban minorities and it's relationship to conduct disorders, depression and separation anxiety. Journal of the American Academy of Child and Adolescent Psychiatry, 36; 75-84.

49. Ferlay J., F. Bray (2000). Globocan 2000, Cancer incidence, mortality and prevalence worldwide. IARC Press, Lyon, International Agency for Research on Cancer, World Health Organisation.

50. Frosh Stephen, Ann Phoenix, Rob Pattman, 'The trouble with boys', February 2003, Vol. 16 No2, pages 84-87.The Psychologist.

51. Garda Siochana, (2001), Year 2001 Crime Statistics, Dublin, Stationery Office.

52. Garda Siochana (1999), Annual Report 1999, Dublin, Stationary Office.

53. Gavigan P, McKeon P (1995) Public attitudes to the treatment of depression in general practice. Abstracts of World Congress of World Federation of Mental Health Dublin.

54. Goldberg and Lewis (1969), "Play Behaviour in the Year-Old Infant: Early Sex Differences," Child Development, vol. 40, no. 1.

55. Hakko H, Rasanen P. ,Tuhonen J (1998) Secular trends in the rates and seasonality of violent and non-violent suicide occurrences in Finland between 1980 - 95. Jamal of Affective Disorders, 50; 49 - 54.

56. Hall JA and Halberstadt AG, (1986). "Smiling and Gazing" in JS Hyde and MC Linn eds. The psychology of Gender. Advances through Meta Analysis pp. 136-158. Baltimore: John Hopkins University Press.

57. Hyde JS, (1986). "Gender differences in Aggression" in JS Hyde and MC Linn eds. The Psychology of gender. Advances through Meta Analysis pp. 51-66.

Baltimore: John Hopkins University Press.

58. Kagan J, (1964). *"Acquisition and Significance of Sex Typing and Sex Role identity."* In Martin L. Hoffman and Louis W. Hoffman eds. Review of Child Development Research, vol. 1. New York: Russell Sage Foundation.

59. Kelleher (2000), An Investigation of 100 Cork Suicides, Irish Journal of Psychological Medicine, 17 (3).

60. Kraemer S (2000) The fragile male. British Medical Journal Vol 321

61. Krug E (2002): WHO Report on Violence and Health, Geneva: World Health Organization.

62. Kunst AE, Groenhof F, Mackenbach JP (1998) Occupational class and cause specific mortality in middles aged men in 11 European countries: comparison of population based studies. EU Working Group of socio-economic inequalities in health. British Medical Journal Vol 316: 1636-42.

63. Levi F, La Vecchia C, Boyle P, Lucchini F, Negri E (2000) Western and Eastern European trends in testicular cancer mortality. The Lancet Vol 357 June 9, 2000.

64. Lindsey L, (1990). Gender Roles: A Sociological Perspective. Englewood Cliffs, N.J. Prentice-Hall.

65. Martunnen M, Aro H, Hendriksson M, Lonnqvit J, (1991) Mental disorder in adolescent suicide. DSM 111 - R, Axes 1 and 11 among 13-19 year olds. Archives of General Psychiatry, 48; 834-839.

66. Mathers (2001), Time for creative Thinking about Men's Health, The Lancet, 357: 9271

67. McKeown K, (2002), Domestic Violence is not a Women's issue or a Men's Issue, but a Relationship Issue, Irish Times, February 8th, 2002.

68. McKeon P, Carrick S (1991) Public attitudes to depression: a national survey. Irish Journal of Psychological Medicine 8; 116 - 12

69. Money J and Erhardt AE, (1972). Man and Woman, Boy and Girl. Baltimore: John Hopkins University Press.

70. Murphy-Lawless J, (2003), Establishing the Rationales for Gender-Specific Strategies to Improve Women's Health: The Evidence from Research, Department of Social Policy and Social Work, Dublin.

71. National Cancer Registry Board, (2001), Cancer in Ireland, 1994-1998: Incidence, Mortality, Treatment and Survival, Report of the National Cancer Registry, Cork.

72. National Research and Development Centre for Welfare and Health. Suicide Can Be Prevented. Helsinki, 1993.

73. NCHD (2004): Figures obtained from National Centre for Hereditary Coagulation Disorders, St. James Hospital, Dublin.

74. Nolan, B. (1990) "Socio-economic Mortality Differentials in Ireland," The Economic and Social Review, 1990, 21(2), 193-208.

75. O'Dowd, T. and D. Jewell (1998) (eds.,) Men's Health

Oxford General Practice Series 41.

76. Organisation for Economic Co-operation and development (2002) The OECD observer: OECD in Figures: statistics on the member countries Volume 2002 Supplement 1. Paris: OECD.
77. O'Shea O, (1997), Male Mortality Differentials by Socio-economic Group in Ireland, Social Science in Medicine, 45(6), 803-809

78. Platt S, Kreitman N. (1984) Trends in para-suicide and unemployment among men in Edinburgh, 1968-82. British Medical Journal 289; 1029-1032.

79. Phillips M. 1999 Feminised Britain and the Neutered Male, Social Market Foundation.

80. Renzetti C. 1991: Women, Men, and Society and Violent Betrayal. Daniel J. Curran, Allyn & Bacon

81. Rey J, (1995), Perceptions of poor maternal care are associated with adolescent depression. Journal of Affective Disorders, 34; 95-100

82. Richardson N, (2003), Masculinities, Health Promotion Department, South Eastern Health Board.

83. Richardson N, (2004), "Getting Inside Men's Health", South Eastern Health Board.

84. Roy A, (1983) Family history of suicide. Archives of General Psychiatry, 40, 971-974.

85. Roy A., (1983) Suicide in depressives. Comprehensive Psychiatry, 24; 487 - 491

86. Sabo D., Gordon D. F. (1995) 'Rethinking men's

health and illness'. In : Sabo, D. Gordon DF, eds. Men's Health and illness: Gender, power and the body. Sage London.

87. Sabo D (1999), Understanding Men's Health: A relational and Gender sensitive approach, retrieved from the World Wide Web on the 9th November 2004, www.hsph.harvard.edu

88. Sacks G, (2002), "When Men's Health Doesn't count", Norfolk Virginian-Pilot, 9th October 2002.

89. Schulsinger F, Kety S, Rosenthal D, Wender P. A Family Study of Suicide. In M. Schou, E. Strongren. (Eds) Origin, Prevention and Treatment of Affective Disorders. New York: Academy Press, 1979.

90. Shaffer D, Garland A, Fisher P, Bacon K, Vieland V (1990) Suicide crisis centers: A critical reappraisal with special reference to the prevention of youth suicide. In FE Goldston, CM Heinicke, RS Pynoos and J Yager (Eds). Prevention of Mental Health Disturbance in Childhood. Washington, DC: American Psychiatric Association Press.

91. Shettles LB.(1961) Conception and birth sex ratios. Obstet Gynecol Vol 18: 122-130

92. Smith L, (2003), Improving our defences against the hidden cancer killing men, The Sunday Times, 20th April, 2003.

93. Stakelum A, Boland J, (2001), Men Talking: A Qualitative Study on Men's Health Beliefs and Attitudes in the North Eastern Health Board, NEHB.

94. Stillion J, (1995), Premature Death Among Males, Men's Health and Illness: Gender, Power and the body, 46-67, Thousand Oaks, CA: Sage Publishing.

95. Strauss M, Gelles R. 1986: Journal Of Marriage and the Family, August 1986.

96. Tannen D, (1993). Gender and conversational interaction. New York, Oxford, Oxford University Press.

97. The European Health For All 2003 database, WHO Regional Office for Europe, Copenhagen, Denmark

98. The European Health Report 2002. WHO regional publications. European series; No. 97.

99. The European Health Report 2002 The World Health Organisation.

100.   The Lancet, (2001), Time for creative Thinking about Men's Health, 357: 9271

101.   The Male Link 2000, Men's Attitudes and Values Research, Belfast, Northern Ireland.

102.   The WHO World Health Report; 2002: reducing risks, promoting healthy life. The World Health Organisation, Geneva, Switzerland.

103.   The World Report on Violence and Health 2002 The World Health Organisation, Geneva, Switzerland.

104.   Thompson D, (2002), "When Men's Health Doesn't count" , Norfolk Virginian-Pilot, 9th October 2002.

105.   Tsuang M. (1983) Risk of suicide in the relatives of schizophrenics, manic-depressives and controls. Journal of American Psychiatry, 44; 396-400.

106.   United Nations Population Division, World Population Prospects, country profiles.

107.   Warren LW, (1983), Male Intolerance of Depression: A review with implications for psychotherapy, Clinical Psychology Review, 3: 147-56.

108.   WHO 1997 – 1999 World Health Statistics Annual

109.   Wilson A. (1998).'Getting Help' in Men's Health (eds.,)

110.   World Health Organisation (1999) The 1997-1999 World Health Statistics Annual; - WHO Statistical Information Service (WHOSIS)